W9-AKV-214

Additional Practice Workbook

Workbook

GRADE 2 TOPICS 1–15

enVision® Mathematics

SAVVAS

LEARNING COMPANY

Copyright © 2020 by Savvas Learning Company LLC. All Rights Reserved. Printed in the United States of America.

This publication is protected by copyright, and permission should be obtained from the publisher prior to any prohibited reproduction, storage in a retrieval system, or transmission in any form or by any means, electronic, mechanical, photocopying, recording, or otherwise. The publisher hereby grants permission to reproduce pages, in part or in whole, for classroom use only, the number not to exceed the number of students in each class. Notice of copyright must appear on all copies. For information regarding permissions, request forms, and the appropriate contacts within the Savvas Learning Company Rights Management group, please send your query to the address below.

Savvas Learning Company LLC, 15 East Midland Avenue, Paramus, NJ 07652

Savvas™ and **Savvas Learning Company™** are the exclusive trademarks of Savvas Learning Company LLC in the U.S. and other countries.

Savvas Learning Company publishes through its famous imprints **Prentice Hall®** and **Scott Foresman®** which are exclusive registered trademarks owned by Savvas Learning Company LLC in the U.S. and/or other countries.

enVision® and **Savvas Realize™** are exclusive trademarks of Savvas Learning Company LLC in the U.S. and/or other countries.

Unless otherwise indicated herein, any third party trademarks that may appear in this work are the property of their respective owners, and any references to third party trademarks, logos, or other trade dress are for demonstrative or descriptive purposes only. Such references are not intended to imply any sponsorship, endorsement, authorization, or promotion of Savvas Learning Company products by the owners of such marks, or any relationship between the owner and Savvas Learning Company LLC or its authors, licensees, or distributors.

ISBN-13: 978-0-13-495377-9
ISBN-10: 0-13-495377-0

7 21

Grade 2 Topics 1–15

Name _____

Another Look! You can make a 10 to help you add.

This shows 8 + 4.

Show 10 + 2.
Move 2 counters to make a 10.

  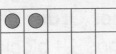

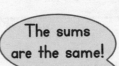

The sums are the same!

8 + 4   is the same as   10 + 2.

8 + 4 = __12__   10 + 2 = __12__

HOME ACTIVITY Have your child use buttons to make a group of 9 and a group of 5. Ask your child to show you how to make a group of 10 buttons to help find the sum.

Make a 10 to help you add.

1. Find 9 + 7.   Move 1 counter to make a 10.

9 + 7   is the same as   10 + ____.

9 + 7 = ____   ____ + ____ = ____

2. Find 7 + 5.

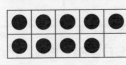

Move ____ counters to make a 10.

7 + 5 is the same as 10 + ____.

7 + 5 = ____   ____ + ____ = ____

Add. Then draw lines to match addition problems with the same sum.

3. 9 + 6 = ____

4. 7 + 5 = ____

5. 9 + 8 = ____

6. 5 + 8 = ____

10 + 2 = ____

10 + 3 = ____

10 + 7 = ____

10 + 5 = ____

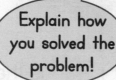

7. Explain Blanca wants to add 5 + 8. Explain how she can make a 10 to solve.

5 + 8 = ____

_____

_____

_____

8. Higher Order Thinking

Jay has 14 blocks in all.
He has 6 yellow blocks.
The rest of the blocks are green.
How many green blocks does Jay have?

Explain how you solved the problem!

Jay has ____ green blocks.

_____

_____

_____

9. Use the ten-frames. Show how to find 7 + 6 by making a 10.

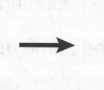
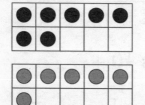

10. ☑ Assessment Practice Which addition problem has the same sum as 8 + 7?

10 + 9   10 + 8   10 + 7   10 + 5

Ⓐ   Ⓑ   Ⓒ   Ⓓ

Copyright © Savvas Learning Company LLC. All Rights Reserved.

Video Tools Games

Another Look! You can use your addition table to find the addition facts that have 7 as an addend.

Find the 7 in the top row of the table.

Write an equation for each sum in that column.

+	0	1	2	3	4	5	6	7	8	9	10
0	0	1	2	3	4	5	6	7	8	9	10
1	1	2	3	4	5	6	7	8	9	10	11
2	2	3	4	5	6	7	8	9	10	11	12
3	3	4	5	6	7	8	9	10	11	12	13
4	4	5	6	7	8	9	10	11	12	13	14
5	5	6	7	8	9	10	11	12	13	14	15
6	6	7	8	9	10	11	12	13	14	15	16
7	7	8	9	10	11	12	13	14	15	16	17
8	8	9	10	11	12	13	14	15	16	17	18
9	9	10	11	12	13	14	15	16	17	18	19
10	10	11	12	13	14	15	16	17	18	19	20

$0 + 7 = 7$

$1 + 7 = 8$

$2 + 7 = 9$

$3 + 7 = 10$

$4 + 7 = 11$

$5 + 7 = 12$

$6 + 7 = 13$

$7 + 7 = 14$

$8 + 7 = 15$

$9 + 7 = 16$

$10 + 7 = 17$

HOME ACTIVITY Have your child practice using an addition facts table by asking your child to write an equation for each sum that is 16.

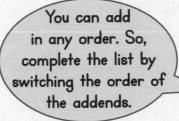

You can add in any order. So, complete the list by switching the order of the addends.

Use fact patterns to complete each equation.

1. $9 + 6 = $ _____

_____ $+ 7 = 15$

$7 + $ _____ $= 15$

$6 + $ _____ $= 15$

2. $0 + $ _____ $= 4$

$1 + 3 = $ _____

_____ $+ 2 = 4$

$3 + $ _____ $= 4$

_____ $+ 0 = 4$

3. $5 + $ _____ $= 6$

$4 + $ _____ $= 6$

$3 + 3 = $ _____

_____ $+ 4 = 6$

_____ $+ 5 = 6$

Use fact patterns to complete each equation.

4. $10 + \underline{\hspace{0.5cm}} = 11$ $5 + \underline{\hspace{0.5cm}} = 11$

$\underline{\hspace{0.5cm}} + 2 = 11$ $4 + \underline{\hspace{0.5cm}} = 11$

$8 + 3 = \underline{\hspace{0.5cm}}$ $3 + \underline{\hspace{0.5cm}} = 11$

$7 + \underline{\hspace{0.5cm}} = 11$ $\underline{\hspace{0.5cm}} + 9 = 11$

$\underline{\hspace{0.5cm}} + 5 = 11$ $1 + 10 = \underline{\hspace{0.5cm}}$

$0 + \underline{\hspace{0.5cm}} = 11$

5. $9 + 9 = \underline{\hspace{0.5cm}}$ $\underline{\hspace{0.5cm}} + 4 = 13$

$9 + \underline{\hspace{0.5cm}} = 17$ $9 + 3 = \underline{\hspace{0.5cm}}$

$\underline{\hspace{0.5cm}} + 7 = 16$ $9 + \underline{\hspace{0.5cm}} = 11$

$9 + 6 = \underline{\hspace{0.5cm}}$ $\underline{\hspace{0.5cm}} + 1 = 10$

$9 + \underline{\hspace{0.5cm}} = 14$ $9 + 0 = \underline{\hspace{0.5cm}}$

6. **Higher Order Thinking** Write 8 equations with 2 addends that have a sum of 13. Use addition patterns to help you.

_____

_____

_____

7. ☑**Assessment Practice** Which have a sum of 19? Choose all that apply.

☐ $10 + 9 = ?$

☐ $8 + 8 = ?$

☐ $9 + 9 = ?$

☐ $9 + 10 = ?$

8. ☑**Assessment Practice** Which have a sum of 15? Choose all that apply.

☐ $7 + 8 = ?$

☐ $8 + 7 = ?$

☐ $9 + 6 = ?$

☐ $5 + 10 = ?$

Copyright © Savvas Learning Company LLC. All Rights Reserved.

Name _____

Another Look! Addition facts can help you subtract.
Use the pictures to find the missing numbers.

HOME ACTIVITY Make up problems during daily activities such as, "If I have 12 eggs and I use 3 of them, how many eggs do I have left?" Have your child write and solve the subtraction sentence using addition facts.

Addition Fact

Think 6 + _8_ = 14.

Subtraction Fact

So, 14 − 6 = _8_.

Addition facts can help you subtract.
Use the pictures to find the missing numbers.

1.

Think 9 + _____ = 13.

So, 13 − 9 = _____.

2.

Think 8 + _____ = 17.

So, 17 − 8 = _____.

3. Lucy had 12 books. She gave 3 books to Michael. How many books does Lucy have now?

3 + 12

3 + 9

6 + 6

___ ◯ ___ = ___

___ books

4. Pam has 20 marbles. She puts 10 marbles in a jar. How many marbles are **NOT** in the jar?

20 + 10

9 + 9

10 + 10

___ ◯ ___ = ___

___ marbles

Think about the parts and the whole.

5. Generalize Subtract. Complete the addition fact that can help you.

19 − 9 = ___

9 + ___ = 19

How do addition facts help you subtract? Explain.

_____

_____

_____

6. ☑ **Assessment Practice** Maria has 11 rings. She loses 3 rings.

Which addition fact can help you find how many rings Maria has left?

3 + 1 = 4
Ⓐ

6 + 5 = 11
Ⓒ

3 + 8 = 11
Ⓑ

2 + 9 = 11
Ⓓ

Copyright © Savvas Learning Company LLC. All Rights Reserved.

Name _____

Additional Practice 1-7

Make a 10 to Subtract

Another Look! You can make a 10 to help you subtract. Find 13 − 5.

One way

Subtract 13 − 3 to make a 10.

Subtract 2 more to subtract 5 in all.

10 − 2 = 8

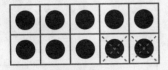

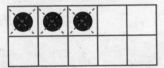

You have 8 left. So, 13 − 5 = 8.

Another way

Add 5 + 5 to make a 10.

Add 3 more to make 13.

10 + 3 = 13

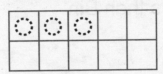

You added 5 + 8 = 13. So, 13 − 5 = 8.

HOME ACTIVITY Have your child use 12 small objects to explain how to find 12 − 8 by first subtracting to get 10.

Use the ten-frames to subtract. Think about the parts and the whole.

1. 11 − 7 = _____

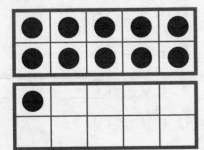

2. 14 − 6 = _____

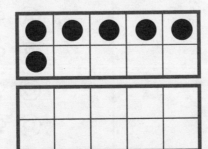

3. 12 − 5 = _____

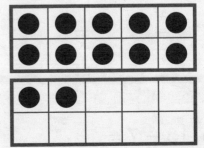

Higher Order Thinking For each problem, pick a bin from each row. Subtract to find how many more bottles are in the bin from the top row than the bin from the bottom row.

A   B   C

D   E   F

4. Bin _____ has _____ more bottles than Bin _____.

5. Bin _____ has _____ more bottles than Bin _____.

6. Bin _____ has _____ more bottles than Bin _____.

7. Bin _____ has _____ more bottles than Bin _____.

8. Make a 10 to subtract. Write two subtraction equations to show how you can find 15 − 7.

_____ − _____ = _____

_____ − _____ = _____

So, 15 − 7 = _____.

9. ☑ **Assessment Practice** Which pair of equations show you how to find 16 − 9?

(A) 9 + 1 = 10, 10 + 5 = 15

(B) 9 + 1 = 10, 10 + 6 = 16

(C) 9 + 2 = 11, 11 + 6 = 17

(D) 9 + 1 = 10, 10 + 9 = 19

Copyright © Savvas Learning Company LLC. All Rights Reserved.

Video · Tools · Games

Practice Addition and Subtraction Facts

Another Look! You can use strategies to help you practice addition and subtraction facts.

Find 12 − 7.

You can think about the relationship between addition and subtraction and use related facts.

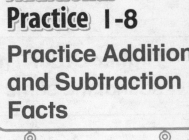

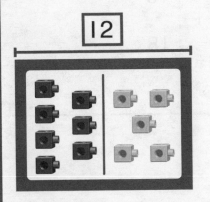

| 12 |

7 plus how many more is 12?

or

$7 + \underline{5} = 12$

So, 12 − 7 = 5.

HOME ACTIVITY Give your child the following numbers: 5, 6, and 11. Tell your child to write the fact family for these numbers as quickly as he or she can.

Add or subtract. Use any strategy.

1.
$$\begin{array}{r} 11 \\ -\ 5 \\ \hline 6 \end{array}$$

2.
$$\begin{array}{r} 12 \\ -\ 6 \\ \hline \end{array}$$

3.
$$\begin{array}{r} 7 \\ +\ 6 \\ \hline \end{array}$$

4.
$$\begin{array}{r} 2 \\ +\ 1 \\ \hline \end{array}$$

5.
$$\begin{array}{r} 12 \\ -\ 3 \\ \hline \end{array}$$

6.
$$\begin{array}{r} 8 \\ +\ 8 \\ \hline \end{array}$$

7. $15 - 7 =$ ____

8. $10 + 9 =$ ____

9. $10 - 1 =$ ____

Higher Order Thinking Fill in the missing numbers so that the sums on the outside are correct.

10.

	3	11
0		3
8	6	

11.

6		10
	9	18
15		

12.

	7	12
8		17
13	16	

13.

6		14
	10	18
	18	

14. What addition doubles fact can help you find $4 + 3$? Explain how you know.

_____

_____

_____

15. ☑ **Assessment Practice** Write an addition equation that can help you find $9 - 6$. Explain your answer.

_____

_____

_____

Copyright © Savvas Learning Company LLC. All Rights Reserved.

Name _____

Video Tools Games

Another Look! You can use counters to solve this problem.

Francine has made 9 wristbands. Jon has made 5 wristbands. How many more wristbands has Francine made than Jon?

Compare the wristbands. Count on from 5 and add to find how many more wristbands Francine made.

$$\underline{5} \; \oplus \; \underline{4} \; \ominus \; \underline{9}$$

You can also subtract. $9 - 5 = 4$

So, Francine has made 4 more wristbands than Jon.

You can use an addition or subtraction strategy to help solve the problem.

HOME ACTIVITY Make up addition and subtraction word problems. Ask your child to use small objects such as paper clips or pennies to add or subtract to solve the problems. For each problem, have your child write an equation to show how to solve it.

Write an equation to solve each problem. Use counters, if needed.

1. 6 bugs are on a leaf.
   2 bugs join them.
   How many bugs are there in all?

   ____ ◯ ____ ◯ ____

   ____ bugs

2. There are 13 baseballs in a box.
   There are 8 baseballs in a bag.
   How many more baseballs are in a box?

   ____ ◯ ____ ◯ ____

   ____ more baseballs

3. **Be Precise** Devin brought his snail collection to school. He has 10 snails.

How could he put them into 2 tanks so two classes could see them?

Write equations for all the possible ways.
One of the ways is given.

Explain how you know you have found all the ways.

$$10 = 9 + 1$$

_____

_____

_____

Write equations to solve the problem. Use counters, if needed.

4. **Higher Order Thinking** Pat has 9 cards.
Frank has 2 more cards than Steve.
Steve has 3 cards.
How many more cards does Pat have than Frank?

Cards Frank has: ____ ◯ ____ ◯ ____

More cards Pat has than Frank:

____ ◯ ____ ◯ ____

Pat has ____ more cards than Frank.

5. ☑ **Assessment Practice** Jan has 10 dolls. Kat has 7 dolls. Choose Yes or No to show if the equation can be used to find how many fewer dolls Kat has than Jan.

$10 - 7 = 3$ ◯ Yes ◯ No

$3 + 7 = 10$ ◯ Yes ◯ No

$10 + 7 = 17$ ◯ Yes ◯ No

$7 + 3 = 10$ ◯ Yes ◯ No

18 eighteen

Copyright © Savvas Learning Company LLC. All Rights Reserved.

Name _____

Video Tools Games

Another Look! Tamra has 8 animal books and 4 sports books. Will she be able to give away 9 of her books?

Solve and explain your work and thinking.

You can also write 8 + 4 = 12 and 12 − 9 = 3. These equations show that Tamara can give away 9 books.

You can use words, pictures, and numbers when you explain.

HOME ACTIVITY Tell your child this story: "Omar has 3 green stickers and 8 blue stickers. If he gives away 5 of these stickers, will Omar have 6 stickers left?" Have your child solve the problem and explain his or her thinking using words, pictures, and numbers.

8 animal books   4 sports books

Yes, Tamara can give away 9 of her books.

Solve each problem. Use words, pictures, or numbers to make a math argument.

1. Alan has 17 stickers. He wants to give 6 stickers to Jean and 7 stickers to Matt. How many stickers will Alan give away? Explain.

2. Tasha has 12 minutes. She wants to jump rope for 8 minutes and play tag for 5 minutes. Will Tasha have enough time? Explain.

T-shirts

The number of T-shirts that four students own is given in the table.

Are there three students who have a total of 20 T-shirts? If so, which students are they?

Number of T-Shirts			
Will	Mandy	Greg	Cindy
4	7	12	9

3. Make Sense What operation will you use to solve the problem? Explain.

_____

_____

_____

4. Reasoning How will you go about solving the problem? Explain.

_____

_____

_____

5. Explain Solve the problem. Use words, pictures, and numbers to explain your work and thinking.

Copyright © Savvas Learning Company LLC. All Rights Reserved.

Practice Video Tools Games

Another Look!

An **even** number can be shown as two equal parts using cubes.

An **odd** number cannot be shown as two equal parts using cubes.

HOME ACTIVITY Choose a number from 2 to 20. Have your child tell if it is even or odd. If needed, he or she can use pennies to help solve.

There are 6 cubes.

Is 6 an even or odd number?

Draw lines to match the cubes.

The cubes can be shown as two equal parts.

$3 + 3 = 6$

6 is an even number.

There are 7 cubes.

Is 7 an even or odd number?

Draw lines to match the cubes.

The cubes cannot be shown as two equal parts.

$4 + 3 = 7$

7 is an odd number.

Draw lines to match the cubes.
Then tell if the number is even or odd.

1. 9 is an _____ number.

2. 12 is an _____ number.

3. 15 is an _____ number.

4. 8 is an _____ number.

$4 + \_\_\_ = 8$

5. 11 is an _____ number.

$6 + \_\_\_ = 11$

6. 18 is an _____ number.

$\_\_\_ + 9 = 18$

Number Sense Look at the pictures. Circle the number you will add or subtract.
Then complete the equation.

7. The sum is an **odd** number.

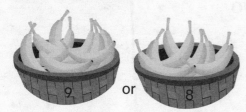

9 or 8

$5 + \_\_\_ = \_\_\_$

8. The difference is an **odd** number.

8 or 9

$15 - \_\_\_ = \_\_\_$

9. The difference is an **even** number.

9 or 10

$19 - \_\_\_ = \_\_\_$

10. Higher Order Thinking Shailen is adding three numbers. He gets a sum that is an even number between 10 and 20. Show two addition equations Shailen could have written.

$\_\_\_ + \_\_\_ + \_\_\_ = \_\_\_$

$\_\_\_ + \_\_\_ + \_\_\_ = \_\_\_$

11. **Assessment Practice** Look at the number. Circle even or odd. Then write the equation.

14

odd   even

$\_\_\_ + \_\_\_ = \_\_\_$

Copyright © Savvas Learning Company LLC. All Rights Reserved.

Name _____

Another Look! The pictures show an even and an odd number.

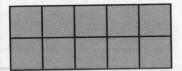 $\underline{10}$ （even） odd

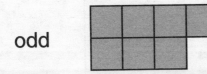 $\underline{7}$ even （odd）

2, 4, 6, 8, $\underline{10}$

Write an equation for each picture.

$\underline{5} + \underline{5} = \underline{10}$

The last top square does **NOT** have a pair.

$\underline{4} + \underline{3} = \underline{7}$

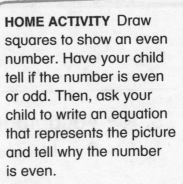

HOME ACTIVITY Draw squares to show an even number. Have your child tell if the number is even or odd. Then, ask your child to write an equation that represents the picture and tell why the number is even.

 Write the number for the picture. Circle even or odd. Then write the equation.

You can count the squares by 2s to tell if the number is even.

1.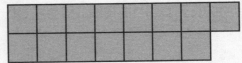

_____ even odd

____ + ____ = ____

2.

_____ even odd

____ + ____ = ____

3.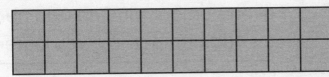

_____ even odd

____ + ____ = ____

Solve the problems below.

4. **Reasoning** Liam says he has an even number of baseballs. Do you agree? Explain. Draw a picture and write an equation to help.

5. 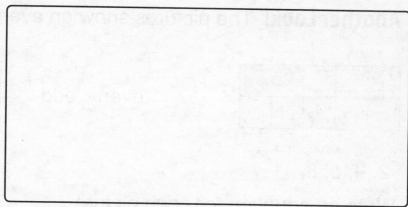 **Vocabulary** Draw a picture that shows $8 + 8 = 16$. Then circle **even** or **odd**.

even   odd

6. **Vocabulary** Draw a picture that shows $5 + 6 = 11$. Then circle **even** or **odd**.

even   odd

7. **Higher Order Thinking** Jacob says that an even number plus an odd number equals an odd number. Do you agree? Explain.

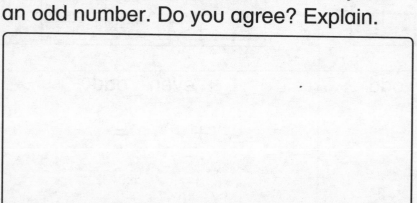

8. **Assessment Practice** How many squares are shown? Is this an even or odd amount?

Ⓐ $3 + 3 = 6$; even

Ⓑ $4 + 3 = 7$; odd

Ⓒ $4 + 4 = 8$; even

Ⓓ $5 + 4 = 9$; odd

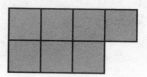

Copyright © Savvas Learning Company LLC. All Rights Reserved.

Practice Video Tools Games

Another Look! You can use an array to show equal groups.

There are 3 rows.
There are 3 circles in each row.

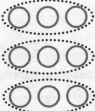 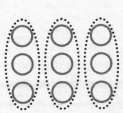

There are 3 columns.
There are 3 circles in each column.

$\underline{3} + \underline{3} + \underline{3} = \underline{9}$

$\underline{3} + \underline{3} + \underline{3} = \underline{9}$

You can add the objects in an array by rows or columns!

HOME ACTIVITY Gather 12 small objects. Have your child make an array with 4 rows and write an equation that matches their array. Then have your child make an array with 2 columns and write an equation that matches their array.

Write two equations that match each array.

1.

By Rows ____ + ____ + ____ = ____

By Columns ____ + ____ = ____

2.

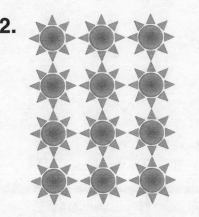

____ + ____ + ____ + ____ = ____

____ + ____ + ____ = ____

Topic 2 | Lesson 3

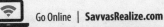 Go Online | SavvasRealize.com

3.  _____

_____

Remember to write the sum.

4.  _____

_____

5. **enVision® STEM** Flowers need bees. There are 4 rows of flowers. Each row has 4 flowers. How many flowers are there in all? Write an equation to solve the problem.

____ + ____ + ____ + ____ = ____

____ flowers

6. ☑ **Assessment Practice** Gail puts her crayons in 3 rows. 5 crayons are in each row. Which equation shows the array Gail makes and how many crayons there are in all?

Ⓐ 3 + 3 + 3 = 9

Ⓑ 3 + 3 = 6

Ⓒ 5 + 5 + 5 = 15

Ⓓ 5 + 5 = 10

Copyright © Savvas Learning Company LLC. All Rights Reserved.

Name _____

Another Look! Make an array and write an equation for the following problem.

Tia places bowls of soup on a tray in 3 columns with 2 bowls in each column. How many bowls of soup are on the tray?

First, draw three columns with 2 bowls in each column.

3 columns

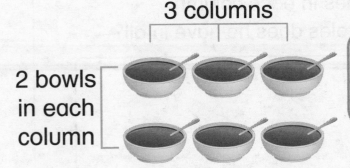

2 bowls in each column

HOME ACTIVITY Ask your child to show how they would make an array for the equation $3 + 3 + 3 = 9$.

Arrays have equal rows and columns.

Now, write an equation that matches the array.

$\underline{2} + \underline{2} + \underline{2} = \underline{6}$ bowls of soup

Draw an array to show each problem. Use repeated addition to solve.

1. Mrs. Smith places the desks in her classroom in 5 columns. She puts 3 desks in each column. How many desks are in her classroom?

___ + ___ + ___ + ___ + ___ = ___ desks

Draw an array to show each problem.
Use repeated addition to solve.

2. **Reasoning** Jim has 4 columns of marbles. He has 3 marbles in each column. How many marbles does he have in all?

3. **Reasoning** Mike has 4 rows of crackers. He has 5 crackers in each row. How many crackers does he have in all?

4. **Higher Order Thinking** Jill has 10 teddy bears in all. If she has 2 columns, how many teddy bears are in each column? Draw an array and complete the equation.

_____ + _____ = 10

5. ☑ **Assessment Practice** Brian has 3 columns of bugs. Each column has 5 bugs. Write an equation that shows how many bugs Brian has in all.

Think about the meaning of the word column.

Copyright © Savvas Learning Company LLC. All Rights Reserved.

Topic 2 | Lesson 4

Name _____

Another Look! You can draw an array and write an equation to help solve problems.

Terri has 3 rows of toys. Each row has 2 toys.
How many toys does Terri have in all?

Equation: $2 + 2 + 2 = 6$

So, Terri has 6 toys in all.

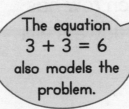

The equation $3 + 3 = 6$ also models the problem.

HOME ACTIVITY Have your child draw an array and then write an equation to model this problem: Joel has 2 bags. Each bag has 3 apples. How many apples does Joel have in all?

Draw an array to help you solve each problem. Then write an equation.

1. Beth has 3 rows of sunflowers in her garden. Each row has 5 flowers. How many sunflowers does Beth have in all?

Equation: _____

_____ sunflowers

2. There are 2 rows of oranges on a table. Each row has 4 oranges.
How many oranges are there in all?

Equation: _____

_____ oranges

Planting Flowers

Mrs. Dunlap is planting some flowers in her garden. She has 10 tulips, 5 roses, and 10 daffodils. She wants to plant the flowers in an array, where each row has 5 flowers. How many rows of flowers will be in her garden?

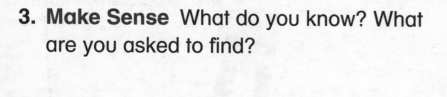

Think about what a row means.

3. **Make Sense** What do you know? What are you asked to find?

_____

_____

_____

_____

4. **Explain** Mrs. Dunlap thinks she should plant the flowers in 4 rows of 5 flowers. Does her plan make sense? Explain why or why not.

_____

_____

_____

_____

5. **Model** Draw an array to show how Mrs. Dunlap should plant her flowers. Label the flowers. How many rows are in her garden?

Copyright © Savvas Learning Company LLC. All Rights Reserved.

Additional Practice 3-1
Add Tens and Ones on a Hundred Chart

Another Look!

Find 16 + 23.

One Way

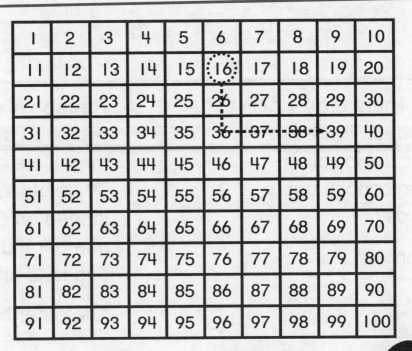

1	2	3	4	5	6	7	8	9	10
11	12	13	14	15	16	17	18	19	20
21	22	23	24	25	26	27	28	29	30
31	32	33	34	35	36	37	38	39	40
41	42	43	44	45	46	47	48	49	50
51	52	53	54	55	56	57	58	59	60
61	62	63	64	65	66	67	68	69	70
71	72	73	74	75	76	77	78	79	80
81	82	83	84	85	86	87	88	89	90
91	92	93	94	95	96	97	98	99	100

1. Start on square 16.

2. Move down 2 rows to show the tens in 2 3.

3. Move 3 squares to the right to add the ones in 2 3 .

4. Where did you stop? 39

So, 16 + 23 = 39 .

HOME ACTIVITY Ask your child to describe how to add 37 and 16 on a hundred chart.

You can also start on 23 to find the sum. Try it.

Add using the hundred chart.

1. 12 + 11 = _____

2. 31 + 45 = _____

3. 81 + 14 = _____

4. $24 + 1\square = 39$

5. $4\square + 31 = 72$

6. $74 + \square 4 = 8\square$

---

7. **enVision® STEM** There are 21 active volcanoes in California. There are 17 active volcanoes in Hawaii. How many active volcanoes are in California and Hawaii?

_____ active volcanoes

8. **Reason** Kenji threw two bean bags at the target. He scored 79 points. One bean bag landed on 61. Which number did the other bean bag land on?

| 53 | 28 |
| 61 | 18 |

The other bean bag landed on _____.

---

9. **Higher Order Thinking** Explain how you could use a hundred chart to find the missing number.

$63 + \boxed{?} = 87$

The missing number is _____.

10. ☑ **Assessment Practice** Which have a sum of 64? Choose all that apply.

- ☐ $22 + 24$
- ☐ $33 + 31$
- ☐ $45 + 19$
- ☐ $54 + 8$

Copyright © Savvas Learning Company LLC. All Rights Reserved.

Practice Video Tools Games

Another Look! You can add two-digit numbers by counting on an open number line. $46 + 27 = ?$

One Way

I can use this strategy to add any numbers.

Place 46 on an open number line.

Count on 2 tens from 46.

Count on 7 ones from 66.

So, $46 + 27 = 73$.

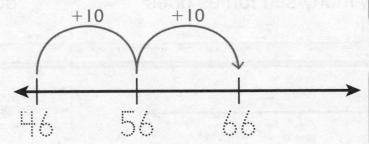

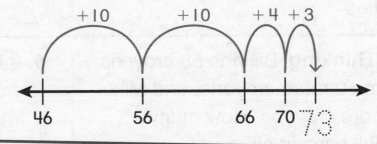

HOME ACTIVITY Ask your child to show how he or she would find $28 + 13$ using an open number line.

Use an open number line to find each sum.

1. $34 + 25 = $ _____

2. $57 + 18 = $ _____

3. Reason Jimmy sees 10 baby sea turtles on the shore. He then sees 23 more baby sea turtles. How many sea turtles does Jimmy see in all?

←————————————————→

_____ sea turtles

4. Reason Ebony has 45 beads. Ivan gives her 26 more beads. How many beads does Ebony have in all?

←————————————————→

_____ beads

5. Higher Order Thinking Bill has 58 crayons. Steve gives him 10 more crayons, and Mika gives him 14 more crayons. How many crayons does Bill have in all?

←————————————————→

_____ crayons

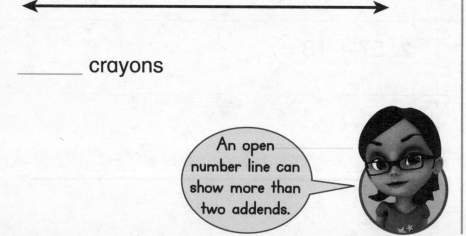

An open number line can show more than two addends.

6. ☑ Assessment Practice Use the numbers on the cards. Write the missing numbers under the number line to show how to find the sum.

| 86 | 60 | 80 | 70 |

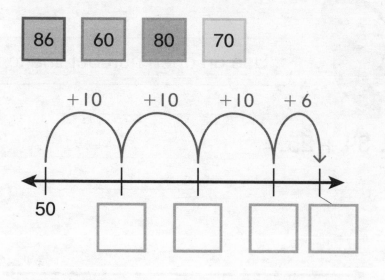

50 + 36 = _____

Copyright © Savvas Learning Company LLC. All Rights Reserved.

Name _____

Another Look!

Find 25 + 34.

Think 25 plus 3 tens and 4 ones.

25 + 34

| 25 | 30 | 4 |

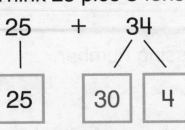

You can break apart the second addend to help find the sum.

One Way

Count on by tens to add 3 tens.

25, <u>35</u>, <u>45</u>, <u>55</u>

Then count on by ones to add 4 ones.

55, <u>56</u>, <u>57</u>, <u>58</u>, <u>59</u>

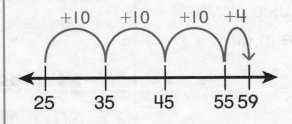

So, 25 + 34 = 59.

HOME ACTIVITY Ask your child to explain how to add 43 + 26 in his or her head.

Break apart numbers to find the sums.
Show your work. Draw pictures, if needed.

1. 16 + 22 = _____

2. 47 + 29 = _____

3. 56 + 35 = _____

Break apart numbers to find each sum. Show your work. Draw pictures, if needed.

4. $14 + 28 =$ _____

5. $26 + 48 =$ _____

6. $43 + 17 =$ _____

7. Break apart numbers to solve. Show your work.

Lily has 46 songs on her music player. Tonya has 53 songs on her music player. How many songs do they have in all?

_____ songs

8. Algebra Write the missing number.

$50 + \triangle = 75$

$\triangle + 25 = 50$

$\triangle =$ _____

$\blacksquare + 38 = 80$

$30 + \blacksquare = 72$

$\blacksquare =$ _____

9. Higher Order Thinking Use the numbers on the cards. Use each number once to make a true equation.

6   7   8

1 ☐ + ☐ 5 = ☐ 2

10. ☑ **Assessment Practice** Which have a sum of 60? Choose all that apply.

☐ $30 + 30$

☐ $35 + 35$

☐ $45 + 15$

☐ $50 + 10$

Copyright © Savvas Learning Company LLC. All Rights Reserved.

Name _____

Another Look! There are many different ways to use compensation to make numbers that are easy to add mentally.

Use compensation to find $47 + 28$.

One Way

- Give **3** to 47 to make 50.
  Give **2** to 28 to make 30.

$$47 + 28$$
$$+3 \quad +2$$

- Then it is easy to add in your head. $50 + 30 = 80$

- You added $3 + 2 = 5$. So subtract **5** $80 - 5 = 75$
  from 80 to find the answer.
  You can count back 5 from 80 to   80, <u>79</u>, <u>78</u>, <u>77</u>, <u>76</u>, <u>75</u>
  check your answer.

So, $47 + 28 = 75$.

HOME ACTIVITY Ask your child to explain how to use compensation to add $17 + 38$ mentally.

Compensation is a way to make numbers that are easy to add in your head!

Use compensation to make numbers that are easier to add. Then solve. Show your work.

1. $26 + 6 = $ _____

2. $17 + 19 = $ _____

3. $39 + 54 = $ _____

Use compensation to make numbers that are easier to add. Then solve. Show your work.

4. 24 + 18 = _____

5. 25 + 27 = _____

6. 43 + 32 = _____

---

7. Use compensation to solve. Show your work.

Wendy found 13 bugs and Wally found 27 bugs. How many bugs did they find in all?

_____ bugs

8. Higher Order Thinking Use compensation to write 3 different equations with the same sum as 38 + 16. Then solve.

38 + 16 = _____

A. _____ + _____ = _____

B. _____ + _____ = _____

C. _____ + _____ + _____ = _____

---

9. 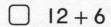 **Assessment Practice** Which are equal to 14 + 8? Choose all that apply.

☐ 12 + 6

☐ 12 + 10

☐ 10 + 12

☐ 10 + 4 + 8

10. ☑ **Assessment Practice** Which are equal to 26 + 16? Choose all that apply.

☐ 30 + 10 + 2

☐ 30 + 12

☐ 25 + 20

☐ 20 + 22

Copyright © Savvas Learning Company LLC. All Rights Reserved.

Practice Video Tools Games

Another Look! Find $24 + 56$.

One Way

Step 1: Remember, $24 + 56 = 56 + 24$.

Step 2: Place __56__ on an open number line.

Step 3: Count on __2__ tens from 56 to get to __76__.

Step 4: Then count on __4__ ones from 76 to get to __80__.

So, $24 + 56 =$ __80__.

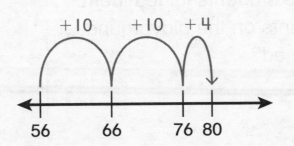

+10   +10   +4

56   66   76 80

HOME ACTIVITY Ask your child to show and describe how to find $46 + 27$ using an open number line.

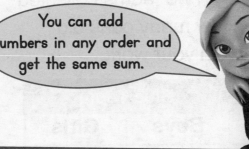

You can add numbers in any order and get the same sum.

Add using an open number line or another strategy. Show your work.

1. $38 + 6 =$ _____

2. $29 + 67 =$ _____

3. $48 + 34 =$ _____

4. **Reasoning** There were 43 students on the playground. Some more students joined them. Now there are 63 students on the playground. How many students joined?

_____ students

5. Roger has 14 grapes. Lisa has 49 grapes. How many grapes do Roger and Lisa have in all?

_____ grapes

6. **Higher Order Thinking** Two teams collected cans for a food drive. How many cans did they collect in all? Explain your work.

Red Team		Blue Team	
Boys	**Girls**	**Boys**	**Girls**
23	28	12	30

7. Use any strategy to find 34 + 49. Explain your work.

_____

_____

8. ☑ **Assessment Practice** Victor used a hundred chart to find a sum. He started at 27. Then he moved down 1 row and ahead 2 spaces.

Which is the sum he found?

Ⓐ 30   Ⓒ 49

Ⓑ 39   Ⓓ 57

Copyright © Savvas Learning Company LLC. All Rights Reserved.

Practice Video Tools Games

Another Look! Write equations to solve two-step problems.

Allison collected 23 rocks.
Jason collected 15 more rocks than Allison.
Phil collected 3 fewer rocks than Allison.

How many rocks does Jason have?
How many rocks does Phil have?

Be sure to solve each part of the problem!

HOME ACTIVITY Make up story problems that take two questions, or steps, to solve. Ask your child to solve both steps of each problem.

Number of rocks Jason has: $23 + 15 = ?$

$23 + 10 = 33$ and $33 + 5 = 38$

So, Jason has ___38___ rocks.

You can count back 3 from 23 to find the number of rocks Phil has.

23, __22__, __21__, __20__ So, Phil has __20__ rocks.

Write equations to solve the problems.

1. There are 4 fewer students in Ms. Jagger's class than Mr. Curley's class. Mr. Curley's class has 20 students. How many students are in Ms. Jagger's class?

   _____ – _____ = _____

   _____ students

2. There are 13 green grapes and 7 red grapes in a bowl. Joe ate 5 of the grapes. How many grapes are in the bowl now?

   _____ + _____ = _____

   _____ – _____ = _____

   _____ grapes

3. ▮ + 42 = 58

   ▮ = _____

4. 33 + 49 = ▲

   ▲ = _____

5. 76 + ⬤ = 89

   ⬤ = _____

Write equations to solve each problem.

6. There are 6 girls at a park. 6 boys join them. Then 4 girls go home. How many children are at the park now?

   _____ + _____ = _____

   _____ − _____ = _____

   _____ children

7. **Higher Order Thinking** Mr. Villa's class has 23 students. Ms. Anderson's class has 3 more students than Mr. Villa's class. How many students are there in all?

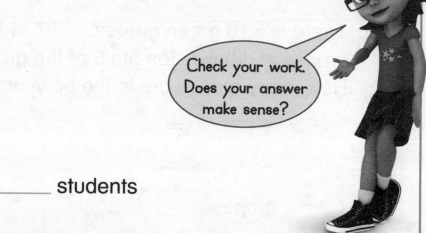

Check your work. Does your answer make sense?

   _____ students

8. ☑ **Assessment Practice** Mike used 27 nails to build a chair. He used 14 more nails to build a table than he used to build the chair. How many nails did Mike use in all?

   Ⓐ 78

   Ⓑ 68

   Ⓒ 41

   Ⓓ 31

Copyright © Savvas Learning Company LLC. All Rights Reserved.

Practice Video Tools Games

Another Look! Solve the problem. Use pictures, words, or equations to make a math argument.

Jamie read 23 pages of a book last week.
This week, she read 26 more pages.
How many pages did Jamie read in all?

23	24	25	26	27	28	29
33	34	35	36	37	38	39
43	44	45	46	47	48	49

I can use a hundred chart to solve the problem. I can start at 23 and count on 2 tens and then 6 ones to add 26. I land on 49. So, 23 + 26 = 49.

$23 + 26 = 49$ pages. Jamie read 49 pages in all.

HOME ACTIVITY Take turns adding two 2-digit numbers. Use drawings of tens and ones to show how you found each sum.

Solve the problem. Use pictures, words, or equations to make a math argument. Show your work.

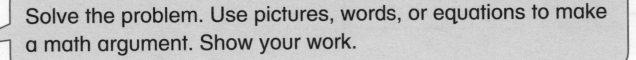

I. A year ago, Maggie's puppy weighed 16 pounds. Now her puppy weighs 37 pounds more. How much does Maggie's puppy weigh now?

_____ ◯ _____ ◯ _____ pounds

Rubber Bands

Juan wants to buy 1 small bag and
1 medium bag of rubber bands. Will
that give him more rubber bands
than a large bag? Explain.

Number of Rubber Bands in a Bag		
Small	**Medium**	**Large**
25	45	70

2. **Make Sense** What information is given?
What do you need to find?

_____

_____

_____

3. **Reasoning** Juan wants to use counters to
solve the problem. Do you think Juan's tool
choice is a good one? Why or why not?

_____

_____

_____

4. **Explain** If Juan buys 1 small bag and
1 medium bag of rubber bands, will he
have more rubber bands than a large
bag has? Make a math argument.

_____

_____

_____

_____

_____

_____

44 forty-four

Copyright © Savvas Learning Company LLC. All Rights Reserved.

Name _____

Another Look! You can use these steps to add. Add 46 + 18.

Step 1: Show the tens and ones for 46 and 18.
Make 1 ten with 10 ones.

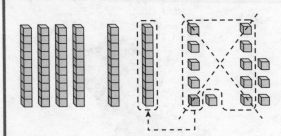

Step 2: Count the tens.
Count the ones.

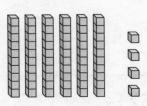

So, 46 + 18 = __64__.

HOME ACTIVITY Ask your child to show you how to add 27 + 34 using place-value blocks. Have your child explain each step of the addition.

Add. Use place-value blocks to find each sum.
Regroup if needed.

1. 24 + 29 = _____

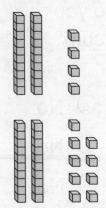

2. 37 + 45 = _____

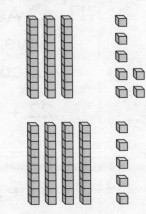

3. 42 + 26 = _____

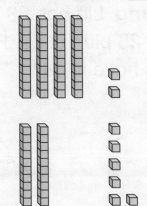

Add. Use place-value blocks to find each sum. Regroup if needed.

4. 57 + 27 = _____

5. 62 + 15 = _____

6. 19 + 33 = _____

Remember to regroup 10 ones into 1 ten if you can.

7. 27 + 18 = _____

8. 23 + 57 = _____

9. 38 + 24 = _____

10. Reasoning Lia has 38 red cups. She has 25 blue cups. How many cups does Lia have in all?

_____ cups

11. ☑ **Assessment Practice** Do you have to regroup to find each sum? Choose Yes or No.

22 + 41 = ?   ◯ Yes   ◯ No

19 + 60 = ?   ◯ Yes   ◯ No

64 + 28 = ?   ◯ Yes   ◯ No

39 + 52 = ?   ◯ Yes   ◯ No

Copyright © Savvas Learning Company LLC. All Rights Reserved.

Name _____

Practice Video Tools Games

Another Look!

Find 36 + 28.

Step 1
Draw the numbers.
Add the tens.
3 tens and 2 tens

30 + 20 = 50

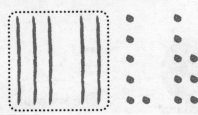

Step 2
Add the ones.

6 + 8 = 14

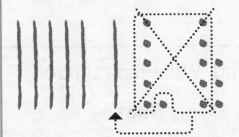

Make 1 ten with 10 ones.

Add: 50 + 10 + 4 = 64

Another Way

   3 tens +   6 ones
+ 2 tens + 8 ones
_____
   5 tens + 14 ones

Regroup
5 tens 1 ten 4 ones

50 + 10 + 4 = 64

So, 36 + 28 = 64.

HOME ACTIVITY Write 27 + 44 on a sheet of paper. Ask your child to draw place-value blocks and regroup to find the total.

Add. Use place value. Draw blocks or use another way.

1. 24 + 35 = _____

2. 17 + 44 = _____

3. 58 + 24 = _____

4. 25 + 65 = _____

5. 53 + 23 = _____

6. 35 + 28 = _____

7. 39 + 48 = _____

8. 69 + 27 = _____

---

9. Higher Order Thinking Draw the second addend. Write the number.

First Addend

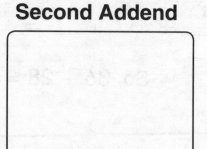

Second Addend

Sum

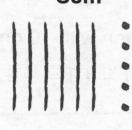

Think about place value when you draw.

---

10. Algebra Write each missing number.

28 + ◼ = 48   ▲ + 18 = 68

◼ = _____   ▲ = _____

11. ☑ **Assessment Practice** Which is the sum of 12 + 17?

Ⓐ 27

Ⓑ 28

Ⓒ 29

Ⓓ 30

Copyright © Savvas Learning Company LLC. All Rights Reserved.

Name _____

Additional Practice 4-3
Add with Partial Sums

Another Look! Find 32 + 45. Use partial sums and drawings of place-value blocks.

Write the problem this way.   32 + 45 = ?

Step 1: Add the tens   30 + 40 = 70

Step 2: Add the ones.   2 + 5 = 7

Step 3: Add the
              partial sums.   70 + 7 = 77

So, 32 + 45 = 77 .

Draw

| | | | | | |

Show each addend as tens and ones.

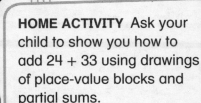

HOME ACTIVITY Ask your child to show you how to add 24 + 33 using drawings of place-value blocks and partial sums.

Add. Use partial sums. Draw blocks if you need to.

1. 23 + 16 = _____

Add the tens.

_____ + _____ = _____

Add the ones.

_____ + _____ = _____

Add the partial sums.

_____ + _____ = _____

2. 35 + 29 = _____

Add the tens.

_____ + _____ = _____

Add the ones.

_____ + _____ = _____

Add the partial sums.

_____ + _____ = _____

Solve each problem. Show your work.

3. Make Sense 28 leaves fell from a tree. Then 32 more leaves fell. How many leaves fell in all?

_____ leaves

4. Liam put 6 cars on his empty toy racetrack. Then Joe put 8 cars on the track. Then Kim put 4 cars on the track. How many cars are on the track now?

_____ cars

5. Higher Order Thinking Write each missing number. What pattern do you see?

$34 + \boxed{} = 44$

$44 + \boxed{} = 54$

$54 + \boxed{} = 64$

6. ☑ Assessment Practice Which is the sum of $16 + 37$? Use partial sums to solve.

Ⓐ 16

Ⓑ 21

Ⓒ 43

Ⓓ 53

Copyright © Savvas Learning Company LLC. All Rights Reserved.

Name _____

Additional Practice 4-4

Add Using Mental Math and Partial Sums

Another Look! Find 34 + 27.

Step 1
Draw the addends.
Add the tens.
3 tens + 2 tens
30 + 20 = 50

Step 2
Add the ones.
4 + 7 = 11

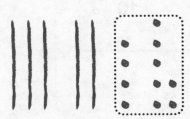

Step 3
Record your work.
Add the partial sums.

	Tens	Ones
	3	4
+	2	7
Tens:	5	0
Ones:	1	1
Sum:	6	1

So, 34 + 27 = 61.

HOME ACTIVITY Write 28 + 45 on a sheet of paper. Have your child find the sum using drawn place-value blocks and partial sums. Once finished, have your child explain his or her work.

Write the addition problem. Add. Use drawings of blocks and partial sums.

1. 18 + 26

	Tens	Ones
+		
Tens:		
Ones:		
Sum:		

2. 75 + 14

	Tens	Ones
+		
Tens:		
Ones:		
Sum:		

3. 31 + 39

	Tens	Ones
+		
Tens:		
Ones:		
Sum:		

4. 37 + 25

	Tens	Ones
+		
Tens:		
Ones:		
Sum:		

Higher Order Thinking Read the sum. Circle all of the number pairs in the box that match that sum.

5. Sum 22

10	4	18
12	15	14
20	21	13

6. Sum 55

25	30	14
18	14	45
15	21	10

7. Sum 83

30	45	30
56	19	64
27	29	20

8. (A-Z) **Vocabulary** Paul has a stack of 47 cards. He also has a stack of 36 cards. How many cards does Paul have in all?

_____ cards

Be precise.

Fill in the blanks.

The **addends** you can use to solve this problem are _____ and _____.

9. ☑ **Assessment Practice** Find $64 + 28$. Use drawings and numbers to show how you solved the problem.

$64 + 28 =$ _____

Copyright © Savvas Learning Company LLC. All Rights Reserved.

Name _____

**Additional
Practice 4-5**

**Break Apart
Numbers and
Add Using
Mental Math**

Another Look!

Find 46 + 25.

You can add mentally! Break apart the second addend in different ways.

Break apart the second addend to make a 10.

Think: What number plus 46 equals 50?

46 + 25 = ?

| 4 | 21 |

50

71

Make a 10.

46 + 4 = 50

Add mentally.

50 + 21 = 71

So, 46 + 25 = 71.

HOME ACTIVITY Ask your child to show how he or she would break apart numbers to find 29 + 46 mentally.

Find each sum using mental math. Draw pictures of blocks if needed.

1. 33 + 16 = _____

2. 35 + 48 = _____

3. 67 + 28 = _____

4. 57 + 19 = _____

Generalize Solve each problem mentally. Show your work. Think about the steps you do every time you break apart numbers to add.

5. $32 + 12 =$ _____

6. $54 + 7 =$ _____

7. $37 + 43 =$ _____

8. Higher Order Thinking Carla buys two packages of pens. She buys 49 pens in all. Which color pens does Carla buy? Show how you found the answer.

Pen Packages	
Pen Color	Number of Pens
Blue	25
Black	12
Red	24
Green	33

9. ☑ **Assessment Practice** Use mental math to find $19 + 43$. Explain why the strategy works.

Copyright © Savvas Learning Company LLC. All Rights Reserved.

Practice Video Tools Games

Another Look! There are different strategies you can use to find $14 + 24 + 36 + 23$.

One Way

Write each number as tens and ones.
Add the tens. Add the ones.
Then add the partial sums.

Try to make a 10 to add quickly.
$4 + 6 = 10$

Tens	Ones
1	4
2	④
3	⑥
+ 2	3
Tens: 8	0
Ones: 1	7
Sum: 9	7

Another Way

Add in any order.

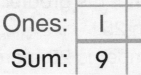

37

$14 + 24 + 36 + 23 = ?$

60

Then add the partial sums.
$37 + 60 = 97$
So, $14 + 24 + 36 + 23 = \underline{97}$.

HOME ACTIVITY Ask your child to find the sum of $16 + 14 + 6$ using two different strategies.

Add. Use partial sums or add in any order.

1. $21 + 10 + 24 + 29 = $ _____

2. $12 + 17 + 24 = $ _____

3. $12 + 15 + 38 = $ _____

4. $45 + 13 + 15 + 22 = $ _____

5. $27 + 22 + 36 = $ _____

6. $29 + 23 + 19 + 11 = $ _____

7. Sum: 83

5   44   12   19   10   20

One number is the sum of 22 + 22.
One number is one less than 20.
One number is greater than 19 and less than 44.

---

8. Sum: 72

36   12   25   7   33   14

One number has two of the same digits.
One number is greater than 12 and less than 25.
One number is 20 more than 5.

---

9. Higher Order Thinking Mac's family donates clothes to charity. Mac donates 16 shirts. His brother donates 14 shirts, and his mother donates 9 more shirts than Mac. How many shirts does Mac's family give to charity?

10. ☑ **Assessment Practice** Find the sum. Use any strategy. Show your work.

$$37 + 39 + 12 + 11 = \underline{\hspace{2cm}}$$

_____ shirts

Copyright © Savvas Learning Company LLC. All Rights Reserved.

Name _____

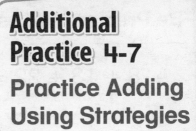

Additional Practice 4-7

Practice Adding Using Strategies

Another Look! Find $34 + 29 + 18 + 6$. One strategy to use is partial sums.

$$
\begin{array}{r}
34 \\
29 \\
18 \\
+\ 6 \\
\hline
60 \\
+27 \\
\hline
87
\end{array}
$$

Step 1: Add the tens in any order.

$30 + 20 + 10 = 50 + 10 = 60$

Step 2: Add the ones in any order.

$(4) + 9 + 8 + (6) = ?$

$10 + 17 = 27$

Step 3: Add the partial sums.

Think: $60 + 27 = ?$

$60 + 20 + 7 = 87$

So, $34 + 29 + 18 + 6 = 87$.

Add in any order. It helps to make a 10. $4 + 6 = 10$

HOME ACTIVITY Write $22 + 33 + 18 + 7$ on a sheet of paper. Ask your child to show you how to find the sum using any strategy.

Add using partial sums or any strategy.

1. $28 + 13 + 7 =$ _____

2. $34 + 26 + 5 =$ _____

3. $31 + 24 + 11 + 9 =$ _____

4. $8 + 13 + 22 =$ _____

5. $16 + 4 + 28 + 48 =$ _____

6. $20 + 6 + 17 + 46 =$ _____

Number Sense Find each missing number.

7. $6 + 13 + 4 + 7 = \boxed{}$

8. $5 + 15 + 12 + \boxed{} = 38$

9. Higher Order Thinking Write an addition story problem with 3 or more addends. Then solve the problem. Show your work.

10. ☑ **Assessment Practice** Find the sum of $25 + 18 + 35$. Use any strategy. Show your work.

$25 + 18 + 35 =$ _____

Copyright © Savvas Learning Company LLC. All Rights Reserved.

Another Look! You can use a bar diagram and partial sums to solve the problem.

There are 33 red cars, 27 gray cars, and 25 tan cars in the parking lot. How many cars are there in all?

Tens	Ones
3	③
2	⑦
+ 2	5
Tens: 7	0
Ones: 1	5
Sum: 8	5

85

33	27	25

__85__ cars

Add in any order. It helps to make a 10.
3 + 7 = 10
10 + 5 = 15

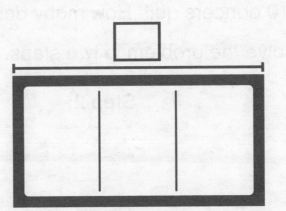

HOME ACTIVITY Write 39 + 14 + 11 on a sheet of paper. Ask your child to show you how to find the sum using a strategy he or she has learned.

Solve the problem. Show your work.

1. On Monday, Matt puts 32 cents in his bank. On Tuesday, he puts in 25 cents. On Wednesday, he puts in 18 cents. How much money does Matt put in his bank on those three days?

Tens	Ones
+	
Tens:	
Ones:	
Sum:	

_____

_____ cents

Solve each problem. Show your work.

2. Alexis has 16 peaches, 18 apples, and 12 pears to bring to school for the class snack. How many pieces of fruit does Alexis have in all?

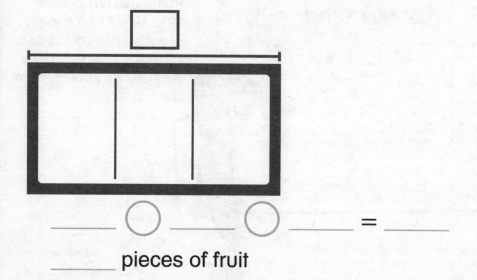

_____ ◯ _____ ◯ _____ = _____

_____ pieces of fruit

3. Higher Order Thinking Chris has 16 party hats. He puts away 9 hats in a box. Then he gets 27 more hats. How many hats are left?

Step 1:

_____ ◯ _____ = _____

Step 2:

_____ ◯ _____ = _____

_____ hats

4. ☑ **Assessment Practice** The dance team has 13 dancers. Then 7 more dancers join. The next week 10 dancers quit. How many dancers are now on the team?

Show how you can solve the problem in two steps.

Step 1:   **Step 2:**

The team now has _____ dancers.

Copyright © Savvas Learning Company LLC. All Rights Reserved.

Practice · Video · Tools · Games

Additional Practice 4-9
Model with Math

Another Look! Complete the bar diagram and equation to model and solve the problem.

Paul has 23 counters.
He gets 27 more counters.
How many counters does Paul have in all?

You can show pictures or numbers in a bar diagram.

HOME ACTIVITY Ask your child to model and find 14 + 19 by drawing a bar diagram and writing an equation.

?

23	27

$$23$$
$$+\ 27$$

Tens: 40
Ones: 10
Sum: 50

$$23 + 27 = \underline{?}$$

Paul has 50 counters in all.

Make a model to show the problem. Then use the model to solve.
Show your work.

Be ready to explain how your model shows the problem!

1. There were 38 yo-yos at a toy store.
   Then the store got 12 more yo-yos.
   How many yo-yos are at the store now?

Go Online | SavvasRealize.com

On the Path

The diagram shows the distances, in feet, of paths between the farm animals.
What is the total distance of the paths from the cow to the chicken, to the horse, to the pig, and then to the cow?

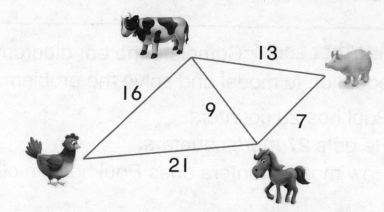

2. **Make Sense** What do you know? What are you asked to find?

_____

_____

_____

_____

3. **Model** Make a model to help you find the total distance in the problem.
Be ready to explain why you chose the model you did.

4. **Model** Use another model to solve the problem a different way. Explain which model you think is better.

Copyright © Savvas Learning Company LLC. All Rights Reserved.

Practice Video Tools Games

Another Look! Here is one way to subtract on a hundred chart.

Find 36 − 24.

1. Start at 36.

2. Move up 2 rows to subtract
   ___2___ tens.

3. Move left 4 columns to subtract
   ___4___ ones.

So 36 − 24 = 12.

1	2	3	4	5	6	7	8	9	10
11	12	13	14	15	16	17	18	19	20
21	22	23	24	25	26	27	28	29	30
31	32	33	34	35	36	37	38	39	40
41	42	43	44	45	46	47	48	49	50
51	52	53	54	55	56	57	58	59	60
61	62	63	64	65	66	67	68	69	70
71	72	73	74	75	76	77	78	79	80
81	82	83	84	85	86	87	88	89	90
91	92	93	94	95	96	97	98	99	100

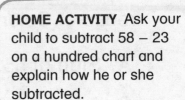

HOME ACTIVITY Ask your child to subtract 58 − 23 on a hundred chart and explain how he or she subtracted.

Subtract using the hundred chart.

1. 87 − 7 = _____

2. 79 − 48 = _____

3. 65 − 41 = _____

4. 99 − 52 = _____

5. 35 − 13 = _____

6. _____ = 84 − 33

Algebra Write the digits that make each equation true.

7. $\boxed{}3 - 2\boxed{} = 71$

8. $5\boxed{} - \boxed{}1 = 14$

9. $78 - \boxed{}5 = 4\boxed{}$

---

10. **Look for Patterns** A treasure is hidden under one of the rocks. Follow the clues to find the treasure. Color each rock you land on.

A. Start at 55.	**B.** Subtract 20.
C. Add 5.	**D.** Add 20.
E. Add 10.	**F.** Subtract 5.
G. Subtract 20.	**H.** Add 5.
I. Subtract 20.	**J.** Subtract 5.

```
 1   2   3   4   5   6   7   8   9  10
11  12  13  14  15  16  17  18  19  20
21  22  23  24  25  26  27  28  29  30
31  32  33  34  35  36  37  38  39  40
41  42  43  44  45  46  47  48  49  50
51  52  53  54  55  56  57  58  59  60
61  62  63  64  65  66  67  68  69  70
71  72  73  74  75  76  77  78  79  80
81  82  83  84  85  86  87  88  89  90
91  92  93  94  95  96  97  98  99 100
```

The treasure is hidden under the last rock that you colored. What is the number of that rock? _____
Describe the pattern you see in the numbers you colored.

---

11. A pan holds 36 biscuits. Kiana put 12 biscuits on the pan. How many more biscuits will fit on the pan?

Ⓐ 24 Ⓑ 23 Ⓒ 22 Ⓓ 21

12. ☑ **Assessment Practice** Which has a difference of 21? Choose all that apply.

☐ 57 – 36
☐ 71 – 50
☐ 86 – 67
☐ 98 – 77

Copyright © Savvas Learning Company LLC. All Rights Reserved.

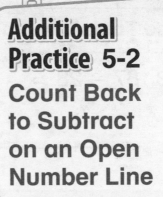

Practice Video Tools Games

Additional Practice 5-2
Count Back to Subtract on an Open Number Line

Another Look! Find 83 − 35.

35

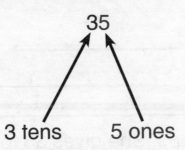

3 tens   5 ones

How many tens and ones do you need to subtract?

First place 83 on an open number line. Then count back 3 tens and 5 ones to subtract 35.

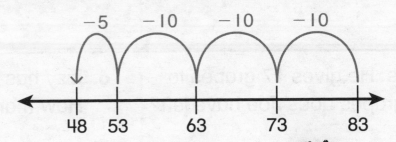

−5   −10   −10   −10

48   53   63   73   83

So, 83 − 35 = 48.

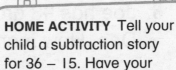

HOME ACTIVITY Tell your child a subtraction story for 36 − 15. Have your child draw an open number line and use it to solve the problem.

Use an open number line to find each difference.

1. 95 − 23 = _____

2. 30 − 15 = _____

3. 87 − 23 = _____

4. 54 − 19 = _____

5. Joe has 43 grapes. He gives 17 grapes to Dee. How many grapes does Joe have left?

_____ grapes

6. Izzy has 99 bottle caps. She gives 33 to Max. How many bottle caps does Izzy have left?

_____ bottle caps

7. Higher Order Thinking Write a story problem for 36 − 14. Draw and use an open number line to solve the problem.

8. ☑ **Assessment Practice** Manuel solved a subtraction problem using the open number line shown. Write the equation his open number line shows.

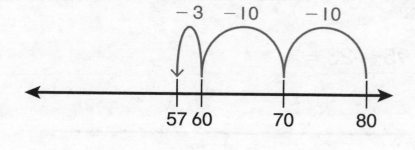

_____ − _____ = _____

Copyright © Savvas Learning Company LLC. All Rights Reserved.

Practice   Video   Tools   Games

Another Look!

You can add up on an open number line to subtract 73 − 45.

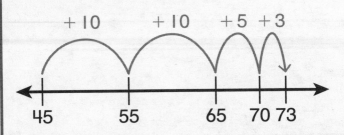

$+10 \qquad +10 \qquad +5 \quad +3$

45   55   65   70 73

You can start at 45. Add 10, and 10 again, to get to 65.
Then add 5 to get to 70. Then add 3 to get to 73.

Add tens and ones to find the difference:

$\underline{10} + \underline{10} + \underline{5} + \underline{3} = \underline{28}$

So, 73 − 45 = 28.

HOME ACTIVITY Have your child tell a story about 52 − 34. Tell your child to solve the problem by adding up on an open number line. Then, have your child write an equation to show the answer.

Add up to find each difference. Use an open number line.

1. 93 − 65 = _____

2. 84 − 67 = _____

Add up to solve each problem. Use an open number line. Write the equations.

3. Use Tools Misha has 36 bows. She gives 19 bows to Alice. How many bows does Misha have left?

_____ – _____ = _____

4. Use Tools Remi has 80 golf balls. He hits 53 of them. How many golf balls does Remi have left?

_____ – _____ = _____

5. Higher Order Thinking Richard found 93 – 67 by adding up on the open number line. Is he correct? Explain. Then write an addition equation to show how you could check his work.

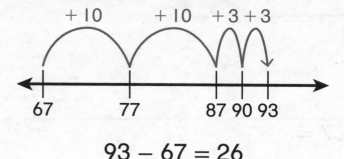

$$93 - 67 = 26$$

_____ ◯ _____ = _____

6. ☑ **Assessment Practice** Use the open number lines. Show two different ways to add up to find 91 – 56.

One way

Another way

$$91 - 56 = \underline{\qquad}$$

Copyright © Savvas Learning Company LLC. All Rights Reserved.

Name _____

Practice   Video   Tools   Games

Another Look! Find 55 – 8.

You can break apart 8 to find 55 – 8.

One way is 8 = 5 + 3.

There is a 5 in the ones place in 55. It's easy to subtract 55 – 5.

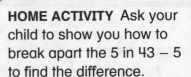

$$55 - 5 = 50$$

Next, subtract 50 – 3. You can count back 3 from 50.

$$50 - 3 = 47$$

So, 55 – 8 = 47.

HOME ACTIVITY Ask your child to show you how to break apart the 5 in 43 – 5 to find the difference.

Subtract. Break apart the number you are subtracting. Show your work.

1. 65 – 9 = _____

2. 24 – 7 = _____

3. _____ = 84 – 8

Explain Subtract. Break apart the number you are subtracting. Show your work to explain your thinking.

4. $41 - 5 =$ _____

5. _____ $= 94 - 8$

6. $25 - 9 =$ _____

7. Higher Order Thinking The table shows how many spools of thread Smith's Fabric Store sold on Monday.

Before the sale, there were 34 red spools and 53 black spools. How many red spools were left at the end of Monday? How many black spools were left?

_____ red spools   _____ black spools

Spools of Thread Sold	
Thread Color	**Number of Spools**
Red	8
Blue	7
Black	6

8. ☑ **Assessment Practice** Ron has 21 comic books. He sells 6 of them to a friend. How many comic books does Ron have now?

Ⓐ 17

Ⓒ 15

Ⓑ 16

Ⓓ 14

9. ☑ **Assessment Practice** Find $93 - 7$. Show your work.

$93 - 7 =$ _____

Copyright © Savvas Learning Company LLC. All Rights Reserved.

Practice Video Tools Games

Another Look! You can use compensation to find 64 − 27.

27 is close to ___30___ .

27 + ___3___ = ___30___

It's easy to find 64 − 30.

64 − 27 = ?
 ↓ + 3
64 − 30 = 34 → 37
 + 3

So, 64 − 27 = ___37___ .

Since I subtracted 30, I subtracted 3 more than 27.

So, I need to add 3 to 34 to find the answer.

HOME ACTIVITY Ask your child to show you how to use compensation to find 82 − 49.

Use compensation to make numbers that are easier to subtract. Then solve. Show your thinking.

1. 65 − 48 = _____

2. 96 − 37 = _____

3. 24 − 18 = _____

4. Make Sense A store had 45 hats for sale. On Friday, 26 of the hats were still for sale. How many hats sold? Think about what you are trying to find.

_____ hats

5. **Vocabulary** Complete each sentence using one of the terms below.

regroup   **subtract**

To find 56 + 38, you can _____ 14 ones as 1 ten and 4 ones.

You can use compensation to help you add and _____ mentally.

6. Higher Order Thinking Use compensation to find 93 − 78. Use words, pictures, or numbers to explain how you found the difference.

7. **Assessment Practice** Use the numbers on the cards. Write the missing numbers to solve the problem.

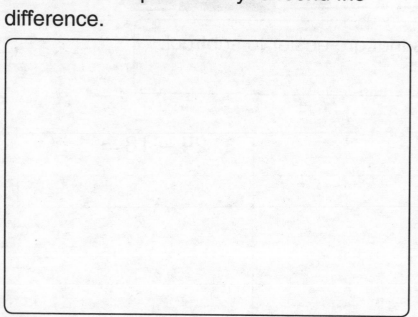

| 2 | 29 | 31 | 50 |

$$81 - 52 = \text{\_\_\_\_}$$

$$\downarrow -2$$

$$81 - \boxed{} = \boxed{} \rightarrow \boxed{}$$

$$\boxed{-2}$$

Copyright © Savvas Learning Company LLC. All Rights Reserved.

Name _____

Another Look! Find 80 − 56.

One Way You can use an open number line and add up to find the difference.

Step 1: Think addition. 56 + ? = 80

Step 2: Place ___56___ on an open number line.

Step 3: Count on ___2___ tens from 56 to get to ___76___.

Step 4: Then, count on ___4___ ones from 76 to get to ___80___.

So, 80 − 56 = ___24___.

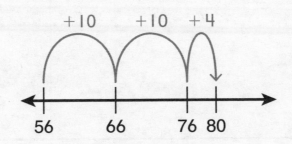
+10   +10   +4
56   66   76 80

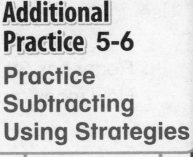
You can solve a subtraction problem by adding up.

HOME ACTIVITY Ask your child to show and describe how to find 46 − 27 using an open number line.

Subtract using an open number line or another strategy. Show your work.

1. 44 − 6 = _____

2. 96 − 79 = _____

3. 82 − 54 = _____

4. Roger has 34 grapes. He eats 19 grapes. How many grapes does Roger have now?

_____ grapes

5. **Reasoning** There were 65 students in the gym. 38 students left. How many students are in the gym now?

_____ students

6. **Higher Order Thinking** Two classes made and sold candles. Which class has more candles left to sell? Explain how you know.

Class A		Class B	
Made	**Sold**	**Made**	**Sold**
33	18	40	21

7. ☑ **Assessment Practice** Find the difference.

$$54 - 27 = \text{\_\_\_\_\_}$$

Explain how you solved the problem.

_____

_____

_____

_____

Copyright © Savvas Learning Company LLC. All Rights Reserved.

Additional Practice 5-7
Solve One-Step and Two-Step Problems

HOME ACTIVITY Make up a two-step story problem for your child to solve.

Another Look! You can solve a two-step problem by writing equations.

Rena counts 6 birds in the tree. 3 birds fly away. Then 8 more birds land in the tree. How many birds does Rena count in the tree now?

Step 1
Subtract to find how many birds are in the tree after 3 birds fly away.

$$6 - 3 = 3$$

Step 2
Add the number of birds that landed in the tree.

$$3 + 8 = 11$$

11 birds

 Complete both equations to solve each problem.

1. Lucy collects 9 rocks. She gives 4 rocks to Sam. Then Lucy collects 7 more rocks. How many rocks does Lucy have now?

_____ rocks

Step 1:

_____ − _____ = _____

Step 2:

_____ + _____ = _____

2. 4 boys ride their bicycles to the park. 6 more boys ride their bicycles to the park. Then 2 boys go home. How many boys are at the park now?

_____ boys

Step 1:

_____ + _____ = _____

Step 2:

_____ − _____ = _____

Solve each problem. Show your work.

3. **Model** Michael put some of the dishes away. Scott put 17 dishes away. They put away 32 dishes in all. How many dishes did Michael put away? Use the bar diagram to model the story. Write an equation to solve the problem.

_____ ◯ _____ = _____

_____ dishes

4. **Higher Order Thinking** Kina picked 14 green apples. Her dad picked 8 red apples. Then they each ate 2 apples. How many apples do they have now? Explain how you solved the problem.

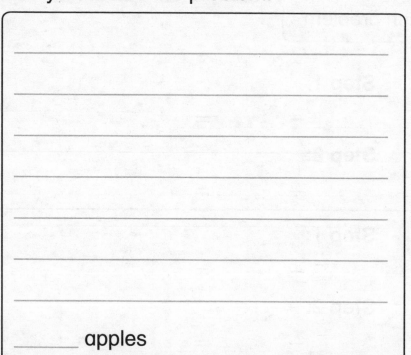

_____ apples

5. ☑ **Assessment Practice** 3 black cats were in the alley. 5 cats joined them. Then 6 cats walked away. How many cats are still in the alley?

Solve. Show your work.

_____ cats

Copyright © Savvas Learning Company LLC. All Rights Reserved.

Name _____

Another Look!

Shane has 62 stamps. Jake has 36 stamps.

Nita says Jake has 26 fewer stamps than Shane, because she can break apart 36 and subtract $62 - 30 = 32$ and $32 - 6 = 26$. Is Nita correct?

$62 - 36 = ?$

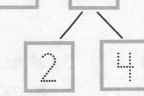

I can break apart 36 into $30 + 6$ and subtract.

$62 - 30 = 32$
$32 - 2 = 30$ and $30 - 4 = 26$
So, $62 - 36 = 26$.
Yes, Nita is correct.

HOME ACTIVITY Take turns writing your own subtraction problems involving two-digit numbers. Make some mistakes in some of your solutions. Then challenge each other to find the mistakes.

Circle your answer. Use pictures, words, or equations to explain.

1. There were 64 runners in a race last year. This year there were 25 fewer runners.

Latoya says 39 runners were in the race this year. She says $64 - 30$ is easy to subtract. So she added $25 + 5 = 30$. Then she found $64 - 30 = 34$, and added 5 to 34 to get 39.

Agree   **Do Not Agree**

Landing Planes

Luis says the number of landings in the afternoon equals the number of landings in the morning and evening. Do you agree with Luis?

Morning

36 landings

Afternoon

74 landings

Evening

38 landings

2. **Make Sense** What do you know? What do you need to do to tell if Luis is correct?

3. **Model** Use pictures, words, or equations to explain if Luis's thinking is correct.

4. **Explain** Luis got his answer by finding $74 - 38 = 36$.

Do you agree with Luis's thinking? Use pictures, words, or equations to explain.

Copyright © Savvas Learning Company LLC. All Rights Reserved.

Name _____

Another Look! You can use place-value blocks to find 42 – 7.

Show 42.

Tens	Ones

Next, regroup 1 ten as 10 ones.

Tens	Ones

Then, take away 7 ones.

Tens	Ones

HOME ACTIVITY Ask your child to show you how to subtract 26 – 7 using small objects such as buttons, marbles, or paper clips. Have your child explain and show you how he or she found the difference.

12 – 7 = **5** ones

42 – 7 = **35**

Subtract. Use the drawings of blocks to help.

1. Find 31 – 5.

Show 31.

Tens	Ones

Next, regroup 1 ten as 10 ones.

Tens	Ones

Next, take away _____ ones.

Tens	Ones

11 – 5 = _____ ones

31 – 5 = _____

Draw place-value blocks to solve each problem.

2. 48 − 4 = _____

Tens	Ones

3. 33 − 6 = _____

Tens	Ones

4. 24 − 6 = _____

Tens	Ones

5. 56 − 5 = _____

Tens	Ones

6. Maria buys 36 beads.
She uses 9 of the beads.
How many beads does Maria have left?

_____ beads

7. Luke buys 7 new pencils.
Now he has 21 pencils.
How many pencils did Luke have at first?

_____ pencils

8. Higher Order Thinking A flag pole is
30 feet tall. A bug crawls 14 feet up the pole.
Then it crawls another 4 feet up the pole.
How much farther must the bug crawl to
get to the top?

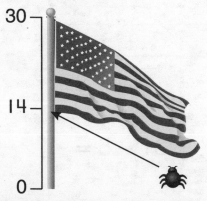

_____ feet

9. ☑ **Assessment Practice** Draw place-value blocks to find 60 − 9. Which is the difference?

Tens	Ones

Ⓐ 51   Ⓒ 49

Ⓑ 50   Ⓓ 48

Copyright © Savvas Learning Company LLC. All Rights Reserved.

Name _____

Another Look! Find 43 – 16. You can draw and use blocks.

Step 1

Draw blocks to show 43.
Take away 1 ten.

Tens	Ones

Step 2

Regroup 1 ten and take away 6 ones.

Tens	Ones
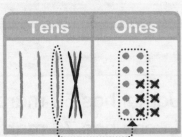

You can regroup 1 ten as 10 ones.

HOME ACTIVITY Ask your child to use paper clips or other small objects to find 54 – 17. Have your child explain how he or she subtracted.

Another Way – Show blocks for 43 and take away.

Take away 1 ten.

Take away 3 ones.

Regroup. Take away 3 more ones.

43 – 10 = 33   33 – 3 = 30   30 – 3 = 27   So, 43 – 16 = __27__.

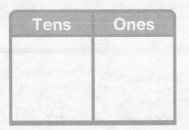 Subtract. Use and draw place-value blocks.

1. 50 – 13 = _____

Tens	Ones

2. 76 – 28 = _____

Tens	Ones

3. 43 – 17 = _____

Tens	Ones

4. 95 – 34 = _____

Tens	Ones

5. 66 − 23 = _____

Tens	Ones

6. 47 − 18 = _____

Tens	Ones

7. 53 − 37 = _____

Tens	Ones

8. 81 − 49 = _____

Tens	Ones

9. Latoya has 95 pennies. She gives 62 pennies to her cousin. How many pennies does Latoya have now?

Tens	Ones

_____ pennies

10. Jamal has 54 marbles. Lucas has 70 marbles. How many more marbles does Lucas have than Jamal?

Tens	Ones

_____ more marbles

11. Higher Order Thinking Ten fewer locks were sold at a bike store on Wednesday than on Tuesday. How many more locks were sold on Wednesday than on Monday?

Bike Locks Sold	
Monday	9
Tuesday	33
Wednesday	

_____ more locks

12. ☑ **Assessment Practice** Draw place-value blocks to find 36 − 17. Which is the difference?

Tens	Ones

Ⓐ 18　　Ⓑ 19　　Ⓒ 29　　Ⓓ 31

Copyright © Savvas Learning Company LLC. All Rights Reserved.

Name _____

Additional Practice 6-3
Subtract Using Partial Differences

Another Look! You can use drawings and partial differences to subtract.

Find 45 – 17.

Step 1	**Step 2**	**Step 3**
Draw 45. You can subtract the ones first. Subtract 5 of the ones to make a 10.	Regroup 1 ten as 10 ones. Subtract the other 2 ones. Then subtract the 1 ten.	Record the partial differences.

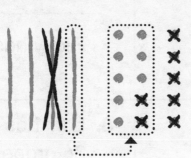

$$\begin{array}{r} 4\;5 \\ -\;5 \\ \hline 40 \\ -\;2 \\ \hline 38 \\ -\;1\;0 \\ \hline 28 \end{array}$$

HOME ACTIVITY Ask your child to show you how to use drawings of blocks and partial differences to find 63 – 38.

Subtract. Draw place-value blocks to find partial differences. Record your work.

1. 37 – 14 = _____

2. 64 – 18 = _____

3. 45 – 26 = _____

4. 73 – 25 = _____

Be Precise Decide which one item each child will buy. Draw blocks and record partial differences to solve each.

Stickers — 14¢
Craft sticks — 36¢
Paint set — 42¢
Crayons — 58¢

5. Bonnie has 47¢.
   She buys the

   _____.

   Bonnie has _____ ¢ left.

6. Ricky has 59¢.
   He buys the

   _____.

   Ricky has _____ ¢ left.

7. Keisha has 62¢.
   She buys the

   _____.

   Keisha has _____ ¢ left.

8. Lani has 63 grapes. She gives 36 grapes to Carla. How many grapes does Lani have left?

   _____ grapes

9. **Higher Order Thinking**
   Use each number below.

   | 1 | 2 | 4 | 5 |

   Write the 2-digit subtraction problem that has the greatest difference. Then solve.

10. ☑ **Assessment Practice** Draw blocks and use partial differences to find 72 – 29. Which is the solution?

   57   52   43   41
   Ⓐ   Ⓑ   Ⓒ   Ⓓ

Copyright © Savvas Learning Company LLC. All Rights Reserved.

Name _____

Another Look! Find 43 − 27. Use place-value blocks and partial differences.

Start by breaking apart 27, the number you are subtracting.

One way is 20 + 7.

You can subtract 43 − 7 first. One way to break apart 7 is 3 + 4.

43 − 3 = 40 and
40 − 4 = 36

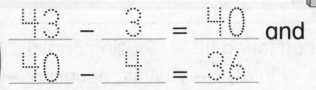

Next, subtract 36 − 20.

36 − 20 = 16

So, 43 − 27 = 16 .

HOME ACTIVITY Ask your child to show you how to use partial differences to find 65 − 38. Have him or her break apart 38 before subtracting.

Subtract. Use partial differences. Break apart the number you are subtracting. Show your work.

1. 76 − 29 = _____

2. _____ = 82 − 39

3. 92 − 16 = _____

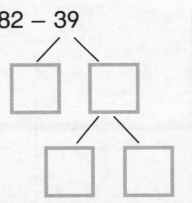
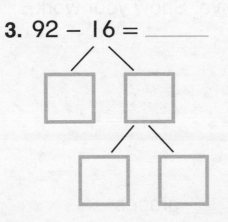

4. 75 − 27 = _____

5. _____ = 61 − 34

6. 87 − 28 = _____

7. Higher Order Thinking Brian found 42 − 19 using partial differences. He broke apart 19 into 12 + 7. Write equations to show how Brian could have found the difference.

How can place value help you solve the problem?

8. Rosita has 55 grapes. She gives a friend 26 of her grapes. How many grapes does Rosita have now? Choose a strategy to solve. Show your work.

_____ grapes

9. ☑ Assessment Practice Can you use the equations to find 86 − 27? Choose Yes or No.

86 − 20 = 66   ○ Yes   ○ No
66 − 7 = 59

26 − 10 = 16   ○ Yes   ○ No
16 − 6 = 10

86 − 20 = 66   ○ Yes   ○ No
66 − 6 = 60
60 − 1 = 59

Copyright © Savvas Learning Company LLC. All Rights Reserved.

Name _____

Another Look! Find 82 – 37.
One Strategy – Compensation

$82 - 40 = \underline{42}$ It's easier to subtract 40.

$42 + 3 = \underline{45}$ Add 3 to the difference.

Another Strategy – Partial Differences

Start by breaking apart the number you are subtracting.

$82 - 37 = ?$

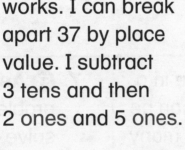

$82 - 30 = 52$

$52 - 2 = 50$

$50 - 5 = 45$

So, $82 - 37 = 45$.

This strategy works. I can break apart 37 by place value. I subtract 3 tens and then 2 ones and 5 ones.

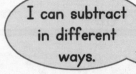

I can subtract in different ways.

I can also explain why a strategy works.

HOME ACTIVITY Write 78 – 29 on a sheet of paper. Have your child use a strategy he or she has learned, to solve the problem. Then ask your child to explain how he or she found the difference.

Use any strategy to subtract. Show your work. Be ready to explain why your strategy works.

1. $56 - 37 = $ _____

2. $46 - 18 = $ _____

3. $75 - 22 = $ _____

4. 45 basketballs are in a closet.
38 basketballs are full of air.
The rest need air.
How many basketballs need air?

_____ basketballs

5. Sue buys a box of 60 craft sticks.
She uses 37 craft sticks for her project.
How many craft sticks are left?

_____ craft sticks

6. Higher Order Thinking 36 berries are in a bowl. James eats 21 of the berries. Then he puts 14 more berries in the bowl. How many fewer berries are in the bowl now?

_____ fewer berries

Is there a shortcut you can use?

7. ☑ **Assessment Practice** Circle the problem that you will use regrouping to solve. Then choose a strategy to find both differences. Show your work.

83 − 45 = _____

65 − 33 = _____

Copyright © Savvas Learning Company LLC. All Rights Reserved.

Name _____

Practice Video Tools Games

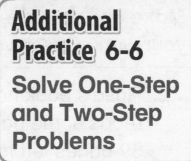

Another Look! 52 cars are parked in the lot. 18 cars leave. Then 10 more cars leave. How many cars are in the lot now?

Step 1: Subtract to find how many cars are still in the lot after 18 cars leave.

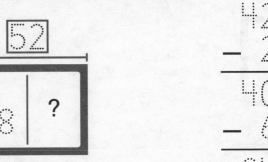

$$\begin{array}{r} 52 \\ -\ 10 \\ \hline 42 \\ -\ 2 \\ \hline 40 \\ -\ 6 \\ \hline 34 \end{array}$$

Step 2: Then subtract to find how many cars are still in the lot after 10 more cars leave.

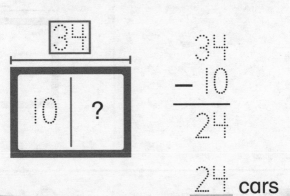

$$\begin{array}{r} 34 \\ -\ 10 \\ \hline 24 \end{array}$$

24 cars

Use the answer from Step 1 to solve Step 2.

HOME ACTIVITY Have your child solve this problem: Some birds are sitting on the roof. Then thunder scares away 12 birds. Now there are 32 birds sitting on the roof. How many birds were sitting on the roof at the start?

Use the answer from Step 1 to solve Step 2.

1. 73 people are on the train. At a train stop 24 people get off and 19 people get on. How many people are on the train now?

Step 1:

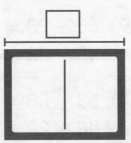

Step 2:

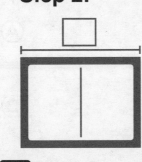

_____ people

Make Sense Make a plan. Solve each problem. Show your work. Check your work.

2. Rosa's book has 88 pages in all. She reads some pages on Monday. She has 59 pages left to read. How many pages did she read on Monday?

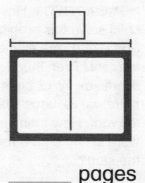

_____ pages

3. Jackie runs 19 laps on Monday. She runs 12 laps on Tuesday. How many laps did she run on both days?

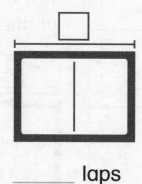

_____ laps

4. **Higher Order Thinking** Zak has a bag of cherries. He gives away 18 cherries to Tim and 18 cherries to Janet. Now he has 25 cherries. How many cherries did Zak have at the start?

Step 1:

_____ ◯ _____ = _____

Step 2:

_____ ◯ _____ = _____

_____ cherries

5. ☑ **Assessment Practice** There are 68 runners in a marathon. 28 runners finish the race. Then 22 more runners finish the race. How many runners have **NOT** finished the race?

Which pair of equations can you use to solve this problem?

Ⓐ $68 + 28 = 96$;
$96 - 22 = 74$

Ⓒ $68 - 28 = 40$;
$40 - 22 = 18$

Ⓑ $68 + 28 = 96$;
$28 + 22 = 50$

Ⓓ $68 - 28 = 40$;
$40 + 22 = 66$

Copyright © Savvas Learning Company LLC. All Rights Reserved.

Name _____

Another Look! Robin collects 36 acorns.
Trisha collects 19 more acorns than Robin.
How many acorns does Trisha collect?

HOME ACTIVITY Ask your child to find 76 − 42 by drawing a bar diagram and writing an equation. Then ask your child to explain what the numbers and symbols mean.

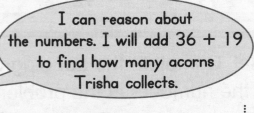

I can reason about the numbers. I will add 36 + 19 to find how many acorns Trisha collects.

This bar diagram shows comparison. The diagram and the equation show how the numbers and the unknown in the problem relate.

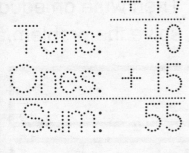

| ? | |
| 36 | 19 |

$$36 + 19$$
Tens: 40
Ones: +15
Sum: 55

$$36 \bigoplus 19 \bigequals 55 \text{ acorns}$$

Reason about how the numbers in the problem relate. Complete the bar diagram and write an equation to solve. Show your work.

1. The Tigers scored 53 points in a basketball game.
The Lions scored 12 fewer points than the Tigers.
How many points did the Lions score?

_____ ◯ _____ ◯ _____ points

Vacation Pictures

Adam, Tessa, and Nicki take pictures on their vacation. How many fewer pictures did Adam take than Nicki?

Use the information in the table to solve.

Number of Pictures Taken

Adam	Tessa	Nicki
19	92	78

2. Make Sense Will you use each number in the table to solve the problem? Explain.

_____

_____

_____

3. Model Complete the bar diagram. Decide how the numbers in the problem relate. Then write an equation that shows how to solve the problem.

4. Reasoning How many fewer pictures did Adam take than Nicki? Explain how you solved the problem.

_____ fewer pictures

Copyright © Savvas Learning Company LLC. All Rights Reserved.

Name _____

Another Look! Jamal has some green apples and 17 red apples. He has 29 apples in all. How many green apples does he have?

You can show word problems with drawings.

You can write an equation with a ? or another symbol for the part you don't know.

12 + 17 = 29, so Jamal has 12 green apples.

29

| ? | 17 |

$? + 17 = 29$

Add mentally.
$17 + 10 = 27$
$27 + 2 = 29$

HOME ACTIVITY Ask your child to write an equation for each of 2 different problems you make up. Then have him or her show you how to solve the problems.

Write an equation with a ? for the unknown to model the problem. Then solve. Show your work.

1. Jill bikes 15 miles in the morning and 17 miles in the afternoon. How many miles does she bike in all?

Equation: _____

_____ miles

2. Maria makes 21 thank you cards. She mails 13 of the cards. How many cards does she have left?

Equation: _____

_____ cards

Write an equation with a ? for the unknown to model the problem. Then solve. Show your work.

3. Model Latisha eats 12 grapes with lunch and then eats some more with dinner. She eats 26 grapes in all. How many grapes does she eat with dinner?

Equation: _____

_____ grapes

4. Model Jack read 24 pages of a book and John read 19 pages of a book. How many more pages did Jack read than John?

Equation: _____

_____ more pages

5. Higher Order Thinking A train has 43 cars. 15 cars are red and the rest are blue. How many blue cars does the train have? Write two different equations that represent the problem. Then solve.

Equation: _____

Equation: _____

_____ blue cars

6. ☑ Assessment Practice 63 boys enter a marathon. 48 boys finish the race and some boys do not. How many boys do **NOT** finish the race?

Write an equation to model the problem. Use a ? for the unknown. Then solve.

Copyright © Savvas Learning Company LLC. All Rights Reserved.

Practice   Video   Tools   Games

Another Look! A bar diagram can help you solve word problems.

Bridget has 15 fewer crackers than Jessica. Bridget has 20 crackers. How many crackers does Jessica have?

Jessica's crackers

?

20	15

Bridget's crackers   15 crackers fewer

Jessica has __35__ crackers.

	Tens	Ones
	2	0
+	1	5
	3	0
		5
	3	5

Bridget has 15 fewer, which means Jessica has 15 more. Add to find the number of crackers Jessica has.

HOME ACTIVITY Tell your child Max has 10 fewer shells than Becca. Max has 20 shells. How many shells does Becca have? Then have your child write the equation. 20 + 10 = 30.

Solve each problem any way you choose. Use drawings and equations to help. Show your work.

1. Ann puts 37 photos in one book and 24 photos in another book. How many photos does she use in all?

_____ photos

2. Jorge's puzzle has 20 fewer pieces than Rosi's puzzle. Jorge's puzzle has 80 pieces. How many pieces does Rosi's puzzle have?

_____ pieces

Solve each problem any way you choose. Use drawings and equations to help. Show your work.

3. **Reasoning** Lucy makes 37 get well cards and some thank you cards. She makes 60 cards in all. How many thank you cards does Lucy make?

Think about what the numbers in the problem mean.

_____ thank you cards

4. **Higher Order Thinking** Jeff finds some bugs. He finds 10 fewer grasshoppers than crickets. He finds 5 fewer crickets than ladybugs. If Jeff finds 5 grasshoppers, how many ladybugs does Jeff find? How many crickets does he find? Write two equations to solve the problem.

_____ crickets   _____ ladybugs

5. ☑ **Assessment Practice** Sandy has 17 fewer hockey cards than Al. Al has 55 hockey cards. How many hockey cards does Sandy have?

Draw a line to show where each number and unknown could be in the equation. Then solve.

| 17 | ? | 55 |

_____ + _____ = _____

_____ cards

Copyright © Savvas Learning Company LLC. All Rights Reserved.

Practice Video Tools Games

Another Look!

Derek has some sheets of blue paper. He has 34 sheets of red paper. He has a total of 67 sheets of paper. How many sheets of blue paper does Derek have?

You know one of the parts and the whole.

$? + 34 = 67$

Subtract $67 - 34$ to find the missing part.

$67 - 30 = 37$ $37 - 4 = 33$

So, Derek has 33 sheets of blue paper.

67

? | 34

Don't forget to check that your answer makes sense!

HOME ACTIVITY Have your child solve the following problem: *Luke sold 27 more raffle tickets than Roger. Luke sold 53 tickets. How many tickets did Roger sell?* Ask your child to explain his or her solution.

Solve each problem any way you choose. Use drawings and equations to help. Show your work.

1. Joshua used 23 more craft sticks on his project than Candice. Joshua used 41 craft sticks. How many craft sticks did Candice use?

_____ craft sticks

2. Gavin painted 14 pictures last week. He painted some more pictures this week. He painted 25 pictures in all. How many pictures did Gavin paint this week?

_____ pictures

3. **Reasoning** Daniel tosses a number cube 19 fewer times than Jayden. Daniel tosses a number cube 38 times. How many times does Jayden toss a number cube?

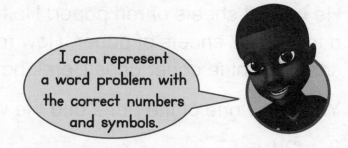

I can represent a word problem with the correct numbers and symbols.

_____ times

4. **Higher Order Thinking** Wyatt has 34 blocks. Stella has 36 blocks. They give 14 blocks to Henry. Now how many blocks do Wyatt and Stella have together?

Complete the steps to solve the problem.

Step 1

_____ ◯ _____ = _____

Step 2

_____ ◯ _____ = _____

_____ blocks

5. ☑ **Assessment Practice** Oliver runs 23 fewer laps than Nate. Nate runs 61 laps. How many laps does Oliver run?

The bar diagram models the problem. Which is the unknown number?

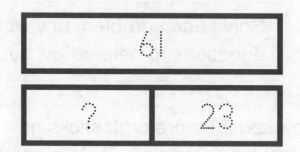

Ⓐ 32

Ⓑ 38

Ⓒ 42

Ⓓ 48

Copyright © Savvas Learning Company LLC. All Rights Reserved.

Name _____

Another Look! You can solve problems in different ways.

Jenna had 13 red markers and 15 blue markers. Then she lost 12 markers. How many markers does Jenna have left?

Step 1
Add to find the number of markers Jenna had in all.
$13 + 15 = ?$

The sum is
2 tens and 8 ones or 28.

Step 2
Subtract the number of markers Jenna lost.
$28 - 12 = ?$

The difference is
1 ten and 6 ones or 16.

I broke apart the problem into two parts. I used place value and mental math to solve each part.

HOME ACTIVITY Make up story problems that take two questions, or steps, to solve. Ask your child to solve both parts of each problem.

$13 \underline{\ } + \underline{\ } 15 = \underline{28} \quad \underline{28} \underline{\ } - \underline{\ } 12 = \underline{16} \quad \underline{16}$ markers

Solve any way you choose. Show your work.
Write equations to solve both parts of the problem.

1. There were 15 red apples and 6 green apples in a bowl. Eric ate 2 of the apples. How many apples are in the bowl now?

Step 1 _____ ◯ _____ = _____

Step 2 _____ ◯ _____ = _____

_____ apples

2. **Be Precise** Three students use the table to record how many jumping jacks they did each day. Complete the table and the sentences.

Hank did _____ jumping jacks on Friday.

Emma did _____ jumping jacks on Thursday.

Tana did _____ jumping jacks on Wednesday.

Jumping Jacks				
	Wednesday	Thursday	Friday	**Total**
Emma	30	_____	15	88
Hank	33	32	_____	85
Tana	_____	35	25	100

3. **Higher Order Thinking** Kendra drew 26 stars. She erased 12 stars. Then Kendra drew some more stars. Now there are 29 stars. How many more stars did Kendra draw? Write an equation for each part. Then solve.

4. ☑ **Assessment Practice** Ken needs to buy 100 nails. He buys 25 nails at one store and 36 nails at another store. How many more nails does Ken need to buy?

Which equations can be used to solve the problem?

Ⓐ $100 - 36 = 64$ and $64 + 25 = 89$

Ⓑ $100 - 25 = 75$ and $36 - 25 = 9$

Ⓒ $36 - 25 = 9$ and $100 - 9 = 91$

Ⓓ $25 + 36 = 61$ and $100 - 61 = 39$

Copyright © Savvas Learning Company LLC. All Rights Reserved.

Name _____

Practice Video Tools Games

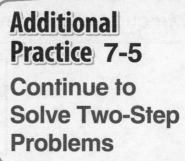

Another Look! Use the answer from Step 1 to solve Step 2.

Tomas has 14 toy cars. Jonah has 6 more toy cars than Tomas. How many toy cars do they have in all?

Step 1: Add to find out how many toy cars Jonah has.

$$14 + 6 = 20$$

Step 2: Add to find the number of toy cars they have in all.

$$20 + 14 = 34$$

They have 34 toy cars in all.

HOME ACTIVITY Ask your child to solve two-step problems. Use small objects found at home as props.

Use the answer from Step 1 to solve Step 2.

1. Dani picked some red flowers and 9 pink flowers for a total of 21 flowers. Then Dani gave Will 5 red flowers. How many red flowers does Dani have left?

Step 1: Subtract to find how many red flowers Dani picked.

_____ − _____ = _____

Step 2: Subtract to find how many red flowers Dani has left.

_____ − _____ = _____

_____ red flowers

Mr. and Mrs. Morley picked their crops. Use the data in the chart to solve each problem.

Fruit and Vegetables Picked

Apples	Peaches	Pumpkins	Corn	Squash
?	23	47	25	17

2. Make Sense Mr. Morley takes the apples and peaches to his fruit stand. He takes 58 pieces of fruit in all. He sells 13 apples. How many apples are at the fruit stand now?

_____ apples

3. Higher Order Thinking Write and solve a two-step problem about the data in the chart above.

_____

_____

_____

_____

4. (A-Z) **Vocabulary** Complete the **bar diagram**. Use two possible **addends** with a **sum** of 25. Then complete the equation.

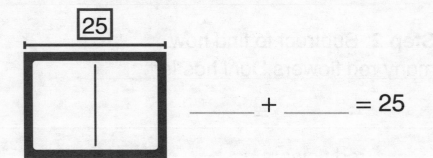

_____ + _____ = 25

5. ☑ **Assessment Practice** 21 students are at the school picnic. Then 42 more students join them. Later, 30 students leave.

Which equations show a way to solve the problem?

Ⓐ 42 − 21 = 21
   30 − 21 = 9

Ⓒ 42 + 21 = 63
   63 + 30 = 93

Ⓑ 21 + 42 = 63
   63 − 30 = 33

Ⓓ 42 − 21 = 21
   30 + 21 = 51

Copyright © Savvas Learning Company LLC. All Rights Reserved.

Name _____

Additional Practice 7-6
Make True Equations

Another Look! Find the missing number to make the equation true.

$$9 + \underline{\quad} = 20 - 5$$

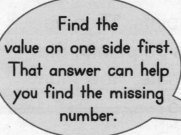
Find the value on one side first. That answer can help you find the missing number.

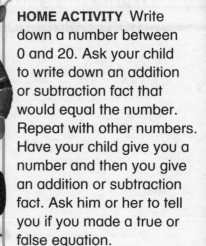

In a true equation, both sides have the same value.

First, find 20 − 5. $20 - 5 = 15$

Next, solve 9 + ___ = 15 $9 + \underline{6} = 15$

So, $9 + \underline{6} = 20 - 5$.

HOME ACTIVITY Write down a number between 0 and 20. Ask your child to write down an addition or subtraction fact that would equal the number. Repeat with other numbers. Have your child give you a number and then you give an addition or subtraction fact. Ask him or her to tell you if you made a true or false equation.

Write the missing numbers to make the equations true. Show your work.

I. $7 + \underline{\quad} = 18 - 6$

$18 - 6 = \underline{\quad}$

$7 + \underline{\quad} = \underline{\quad}$

2. $2 + 4 = 16 - \underline{\quad}$

$2 + 4 = \underline{\quad}$

$\underline{\quad} = 16 - \underline{\quad}$

Write an equation to show each problem. Then solve.
Show your work.

3. **Reasoning** Greg had 6 points. Then he got 9 more points. Joy has 10 points. She wants the game to end in a tie. How many more points does Joy need?

_____ more

4. **Reasoning** Ella has the same number of acorns as Frank. Ella has 9 in one hand and 10 in the other hand. Frank has 8 in one hand. How many acorns does Frank have in the other hand?

_____ acorns

5. **Higher Order Thinking** Write the missing number that makes the equation true. Use pictures or words to explain how you know.

$13 + 4 = 18 -$ _____

6. ☑ **Assessment Practice** Circle the number that will make the equation true.

1   2   3   4   5   6   7   8

$4 +$ _____ $= 1 + 8$

Copyright © Savvas Learning Company LLC. All Rights Reserved.

Practice Video Tools Games

Another Look! Find the missing number that makes this equation true.

$$15 + 10 + 10 = 40 - \underline{\quad}$$

The = sign means that both sides of the equation have the same value.

First, find the value of the side with no missing number.

$$15 + 10 + 10$$

$$25 + 10 = 35$$

Then use that value to find the missing number.

$$35 = 40 - ?$$

Think: $35 + ? = 40$

$$35 + \underline{5} = 40$$

So, $15 + 10 + 10 = 40 - \underline{5}$.

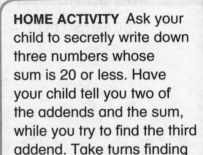

HOME ACTIVITY Ask your child to secretly write down three numbers whose sum is 20 or less. Have your child tell you two of the addends and the sum, while you try to find the third addend. Take turns finding each other's unknown number.

Write the missing numbers to make the equations true. Show your work.

1. $45 - 10 = 10 + 5 + \underline{\quad}$

   $45 - 10 = \underline{\quad}$

   $35 = 10 + 5 + \underline{\quad}$

   So, $45 - 10 = 10 + 5 + \underline{\quad}$.

2. $14 + 10 + 6 = 40 - \underline{\quad}$

   $14 + 10 + 6 = \underline{\quad}$

   $30 = 40 - \underline{\quad}$

   So, $14 + 10 + 6 = 40 - \underline{\quad}$.

Write an equation to show each problem. Then solve. Show your work.

3. **Reasoning** Kris had 22 stickers and got 16 more. Matt had 18 stickers. Then he got some more stickers. Now they both have the same number of stickers. How many stickers did Matt get?

_____ stickers

4. **Reasoning** Lee and Dan have the same number of blocks. Lee has 20 green blocks and 36 blue blocks. Dan has 13 green blocks, 23 blue blocks, and some red blocks. How many red blocks does Dan have?

_____ red blocks

5. **Higher Order Thinking** Jodi has the number cards 19, 10, and 21. Jeff has two cards with the same sum as Jodi. One of his cards is 33. What other card does Jeff have?

Write an equation to show and solve the problem.

6. ☑ **Assessment Practice** Match each number with the equation it is missing from.

$4 + 12 + 5 = 39 -$ _____   24

_____ $+ 14 = 7 + 7 + 20$ 18

$28 + 10 + 10 =$ _____ $+ 24$ 20

_____ $+ 16 = 26 + 10 + 10$ 30

Copyright © Savvas Learning Company LLC. All Rights Reserved.

Practice Video Tools Games

Another Look! You can write a number story about each problem. Then complete the equation to match the story.

$$22 - 15 = ?$$

There are __22__ red buttons.

There are __15__ blue buttons.
How many more red buttons are there than blue buttons?

$$22 - 15 = \underline{7}$$

So, there are __7__ more red buttons.

$$36 - 17 = ?$$

__36__ grapes are on the table.

__17__ are red and the rest are green.
How many grapes are green?

$$36 - 17 = \underline{19}$$

So, __19__ grapes are green.

HOME ACTIVITY Write problems such as $41 - 28 = ?$ and $55 + 37 = ?$. Ask your child to write or say a number story about the problem. Have your child complete the equation to match the story.

Write a number story to show the problem. Complete the equation to match your story.

1. $31 - 8 = $ _____

_____

_____

_____

2. $23 + 37 = $ _____

_____

_____

_____

Bakery Muffins

The picture at the right shows information about muffins at Herb's Bakery. Use the picture to write and solve number story problems.

Herb's Bakery

33 Berry   18 Bran   29 Apple

3. **Reasoning** Write an addition story about the muffins at the bakery.

_____

_____

_____

4. **Reasoning** Write a subtraction story about the muffins at the bakery.

_____

_____

_____

5. **Model** Write an equation for each number story that you wrote in Item 3 and Item 4. Then solve any way you choose. Show your work.

Copyright © Savvas Learning Company LLC. All Rights Reserved.

Name _____

Another Look! You can count on to find the total value of a group of coins.

Joy has 1 quarter and 2 nickels. How many cents does Joy have?

Start with 25¢. Count on by fives.

Think: 25¢   5¢ more   5¢ more

25¢   30¢   35¢

Bo has 1 half-dollar and 2 dimes. How many cents does Bo have?

Start with 50¢. Count on by tens.

Think: 50¢   10¢ more   10¢ more

50¢   60¢   70¢

HOME ACTIVITY Show your child 5 coins. Ask your child to find the total value and write that amount with a cent symbol.

 Count on to find each total value.

1. Sarah has these coins. How many cents does Sarah have?

                    →   Total

10¢   ____   ____   ____   ____

2. Marc has these coins. How many cents does Marc have?

               →   Total

____   ____   ____   ____   ____

3. **Higher Order Thinking** Find the fewest coins needed to buy each toy. Write how many of each coin to use.

Count on as you use each coin.

67¢				
82¢				
46¢				

4. ☑ **Assessment Practice** Which shows 37¢? Choose all that apply.

☐ quarter, dime, penny, penny

☐ quarter, penny, penny

☐ dime, dime, dime, penny, penny

☐ quarter, nickel, nickel, penny, penny

5. ☑ **Assessment Practice** Jamal has these coins.

He needs 85¢ to buy a toy car.
How many more cents does Jamal need?
Draw the coin or coins he needs.

Copyright © Savvas Learning Company LLC. All Rights Reserved.

Topic 8 | Lesson 1

Name _____

Another Look! Victor has 38¢ in his piggy bank. His uncle gives him 2 dimes and a nickel. How much money does Victor have now?

Step I Find the total value of the coins Victor's uncle gives him.

Think: 10 + 10 + 5

10¢   20¢   25¢

Step 2 Add the amount Victor has in his piggy bank with the amount his uncle gives him.

38¢ + 25¢ = ___63___ ¢

So, Victor has 63¢ now.

HOME ACTIVITY Have your child take 4 coins from a cup of mixed coins and count on to find the value. Ask your child to record the value with a cent symbol.

Solve each problem any way you choose. Show your work.

1. Jason has 59¢ in his wallet. His sister gives him 4 nickels. How much money does Jason have now?

_____ ¢

2. Kendra buys a pencil for 18¢. She pays for it with I quarter. How much change should Kendra get?

_____ ¢

3. Megan had 50¢. She lost
1 nickel.
Circle the 5 coins that show
how much she has left.

4. Yoshi had 55¢. He gave
his sister a dime.
Circle the 3 coins that show
how much he has left.

5. Kayla had 60¢. She gave
her brother 4 pennies.
Circle the 3 coins that show
how much she has left.

6. **A-Z** **Vocabulary** Circle the **nickel**. Put a
square around the **half-dollar**. What is the
total value of all the money?

_____ ¢

7. ☑ **Assessment Practice** Tiffany buys
a stuffed animal for 84¢. She pays with
8 dimes and 1 nickel. Which shows how
much change Tiffany should get?

Ⓐ

Ⓒ

Ⓑ

Ⓓ

Copyright © Savvas Learning Company LLC. All Rights Reserved.

Name _____

Another Look! What is the total value of the dollar bills shown below?

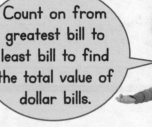

Count on from greatest bill to least bill to find the total value of dollar bills.

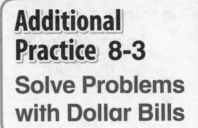

HOME ACTIVITY Have your child make different groups of dollar bills that total $37.

$20 $30 $40 $45 $46

20 + 10 + 10 + 5 + 1

Solve each problem.

1. Ms. Lopez has these dollar bills. Count on to find the total value.

_____

2. Ms. Lenz has these dollar bills. Count on to find the total value.

_____

3. Jack buys a bicycle on sale for $59. Draw dollar bills that he could use to pay for the bike.

4. Look for Patterns Marvin counts six $5 bills. Write each value that he counts. What pattern do you see in the ones digits of the values he counts?

_____

_____

_____

_____

5. Higher Order Thinking Maria has two $20 bills, three $5 bills, and four $1 bills. What other bill or bills does she need to buy a present that costs $69?

6. ☑ Assessment Practice The dollar bills below show the money that Sam has saved.

How much money has Sam saved?

$52 $43 $42 $5

Ⓐ   Ⓑ   Ⓒ

Copyright © Savvas Learning Company LLC. All Rights Reserved.

Practice Video Tools Games

Another Look! Kim has $4 in her bank.
She needs $20 to buy the gift she picked out for her mom.
How much more money does Kim need?

$20 − $4 = ?

You can add up to find the difference.

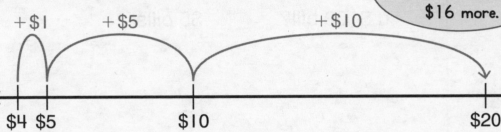

+$1   +$5   +$10

$4 $5 $10 $20

$4 + $16 = $20
That means Kim needs
$16 more.

$1 + $5 + $10 = $16 So, $20 − $4 = $ 16 .

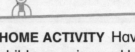

HOME ACTIVITY Have your child use coins and bills to show various amounts in different ways.

Solve each problem any way you choose. Show your work.

1. Mrs. Brown had $16 in her wallet. After shopping at the store, she now has $8. How much money did Mrs. Brown spend at the store?

$ _____

2. Evelyn has $7. Liz gives her one $5 bill and two $1 bills. How much money does Evelyn have now?

$ _____

Solve each problem. Show your work.

3. **Be Precise** Aiden has three $20 bills and two $10 bills. He wants to save a total of $95. How much more money does he need? What bills could they be?

_____

_____

4. Zabrina has a bag with $5 bills in it. How many $5 bills have the same value as:

a $10 bill? _____ $5 bills

a $20 bill? _____ $5 bills

a $100 bill? _____ $5 bills

5. **Higher Order Thinking** Mark has $24. His brother has $8 more than Mark has. How much do they have in all?

Step 1

$_____ ◯ $_____ = $_____

Step 2

$_____ ◯ $_____ = $_____

Mark and his brother have $_____ in all.

6. ☑ **Assessment Practice** Emma has two $10 bills, three $5 bills, and two $1 bills. How much more money does she need to buy a $45 game? Explain.

_____

_____

What bills can you use to show how much more money Emma needs?

_____

_____

Copyright © Savvas Learning Company LLC. All Rights Reserved.

Name _____

Another Look! Show three ways to make 30¢.
Two ways are shown in the table.

Use coins to help you find a
third way. Show 1 dime.
Make 1 tally mark.
How many nickels do you
need to add 20¢?

4

Make 4 tally marks.

Ways to Show 30¢			
Quarter	Dime	Nickel	Total
I		I	30¢
	II	II	30¢
	I	IIII	30¢

HOME ACTIVITY Ask
your child to use quarters,
nickels, and dimes to show
all the ways to make 70¢
with those coins.

Use reasoning to solve each problem.

1. Show three ways to make 10¢.
   Use tally marks to record the coins.

Ways to Show 10¢			
Dime	Nickel	Penny	Total

2. What is the least number of coins you
   could use to make 45¢?
   Make a table, if needed.

   Number of coins: _____

   Coins I would use: _____

   _____

Least Number of Coins

The Williams family wants to buy these toys. They have pennies, nickels, dimes, and quarters. They want to use the least number of coins to pay for each item.

Which coins will they use to pay for each item?

3. **Explain** Marci thinks the family should use three nickels and three pennies to buy the doll. Does Marci's way use the least number of coins? Explain.

4. **Generalize** How can you find the least number of coins to use to pay for any of the 3 items?

5. **Reasoning** Complete the Williams's shopping card. Record the least number of coins they could use to pay for each item. Use tally marks.

Item	Quarter	Dime	Nickel	Penny
Bicycle				
Doll				
Basketball				

Copyright © Savvas Learning Company LLC. All Rights Reserved.

Name _____

Another Look! You can use two kinds of clocks to tell time.

The minute hand moves from mark to mark in 1 minute.
There are 5 moves between each number. So, the minute hand moves from number to number in 5 minutes.

There are 30 minutes in a half hour and 60 minutes in an hour.
The hour hand moves from number to number every 60 minutes.

HOME ACTIVITY Draw three clock faces showing 3:20, 10:50, and 7:05. Have your child tell you the time each clock shows.

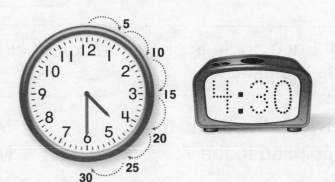

Count by 5s. Write the time.

1.

2.

3. Be Precise The time is shown on the clock below.

Draw the time on the clock in the box at the right. Then complete each sentence.

The minute hand is pointing to the _____.

The hour hand is between _____ and _____.

Higher Order Thinking Each riddle is about a different clock. Solve the riddle and write the time.

4. My hour hand is between the 3 and the 4. My minute hand is pointing to the 7.

What time do I show? _____

5. My hour hand is between the 5 and the 6. My minute hand is pointing to the 4.

What time do I show? _____

6. My hour hand is between the 11 and the 12. My minute hand is pointing to the 3.

What time do I show? _____

7. My hour hand is between the 1 and the 2. My minute hand is pointing to the 9.

What time do I show? _____

8. ☑ **Assessment Practice** What time does the clock show?

Ⓐ 5:00

Ⓒ 5:10

Ⓑ 5:05

Ⓓ 5:25

Copyright © Savvas Learning Company LLC. All Rights Reserved.

Practice Video Tools Games

Another Look! Here are different ways to say time before and after the hour.

6:15

15 minutes after 6 or quarter past 6

6:30

30 minutes after 6 or half past 6

6:45

45 minutes after 6 or quarter to 7

2:40

20 minutes before 3 or 40 minutes after 2

HOME ACTIVITY Draw several clock faces. Have your child draw the time for 7:15, 2:30, and 5:45. Then have your child say the time using the terms *quarter past, half past,* and *quarter to.*

Count by 5s to tell the time. Write the time on the line below the clock. Then write the missing numbers.

1.

___30___ minutes after _____

or half past _____

_____

2.

_____ minutes after _____ or

_____ minutes before _____

3. The time is 6:10. Is the hour hand pointing closer to 6 or 7? Explain your reasoning.

---

4. Nancy arrives at 10 minutes before 8.

School starts at

Is Nancy early or late for school?

_____

_____

---

5. Sean arrives at quarter to 7.

Dinner starts at

Is Sean early or late for dinner?

_____

_____

---

6. ☑ **Assessment Practice** Joyce arrives at school at 10 minutes to 8. Which clock shows this time?

Ⓐ   Ⓑ   Ⓒ   Ⓓ

Copyright © Savvas Learning Company LLC. All Rights Reserved.

Name _____

Another Look! Circle a.m. or p.m. to tell when each activity takes place.

Mom goes swimming in the morning.

I go to soccer practice after school.

Dad goes for a walk after dinner in the evening.

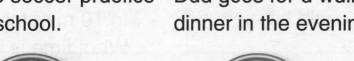

9:15

4:00

6:45

a.m.   p.m.

a.m.   p.m.

a.m.   p.m.

a.m. means before noon. p.m. means after noon.

HOME ACTIVITY Write three things that you do at different times of the day. Have your child tell you whether you do these things in the a.m. or the p.m.

 Complete the clocks so both clocks show the same time. Circle a.m. or p.m. to tell when each activity takes place.

1. Eat a snack in the morning

10:15

a.m.   p.m.

2. Brush your teeth after lunch

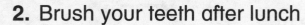

:

a.m.   p.m.

Solve each problem.

3.  **Vocabulary** Write an example of an event that could happen in the **a.m.** Write an example of an event that could happen in the **p.m.**

_____

_____

_____

4. **Higher Order Thinking** Guess what time it is. Right now, it is p.m.

In 10 minutes it will be a.m.
What time is it now? Explain.

_____

_____

Write the time on the clock.

5. ✅ **Assessment Practice** Alexis wakes up in the morning at the time shown on the clock. What time does Alexis wake up?

Ⓐ 7:15 a.m.

Ⓑ 8:15 a.m.

Ⓒ 7:15 p.m.

Ⓓ 8:15 p.m.

6. ✅ **Assessment Practice** Circle a.m. or p.m. to tell when you would do each activity.

Watch the sunset	a.m.	p.m.
Eat breakfast	a.m.	p.m.
Walk home from school	a.m.	p.m.
Take the bus to school	a.m.	p.m.

Copyright © Savvas Learning Company LLC. All Rights Reserved.

Name _____

Another Look! You can show hundreds with models.

Circle the models to show 500.

500 equals ___5___ hundreds, 0 tens, and 0 ones.

Count by 100s to find 500.

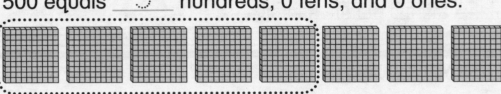

Remember that 10 ones = 1 ten , 10 tens = 1 hundred

and 10 hundreds = 1 thousand .

HOME ACTIVITY Ask your child to count by hundreds to solve the following problem. *Each box of paper clips has one hundred paper clips. Joe has 6 boxes of paper clips. How many paper clips does Joe have in all?*

 Circle the models to show each number. Write the number of hundreds.

1. 200   How many hundreds? _____

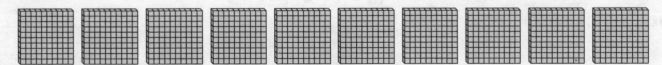

2. 700   How many hundreds? _____

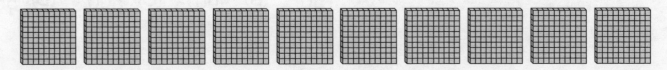

3. 900   How many hundreds? _____

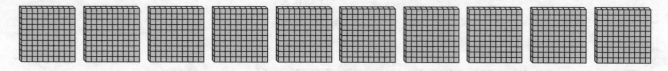

4. 1,000   How many hundreds? _____

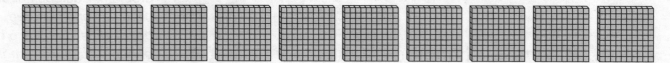

Solve each problem below.

5. Use tens blocks to build 100. Think about how many tens make 100. Draw a picture of your model.

6. Higher Order Thinking Patrick picked two numbers. The first number has 7 hundreds, 0 tens, and 0 ones. The second number has 2 fewer hundreds than the first number. Which two numbers did Patrick pick?

Patrick's numbers are _____

and _____.

7. ☑ **Assessment Practice** Each bag has 100 pretzels. Count by hundreds to find the total. Which is the total number of pretzels in the bags?

Ⓐ 150   Ⓑ 400   Ⓒ 500   Ⓓ 550

Copyright © Savvas Learning Company LLC. All Rights Reserved.

Name _____

Another Look! Use models and your workmat to sort and count.

First, put the hundreds flats on your mat. Next, put the tens rods on your mat. Last, put the ones cubes on your mat.

Write the number of hundreds, tens, and ones.

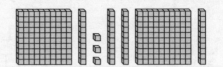

Hundreds	Tens	Ones
2	4	3

HOME ACTIVITY Give your child 50 paper clips or other small, countable objects. Ask your child to sort the clips into 10s and then write the number he or she counts.

Write the numbers shown. Use place-value blocks and your workmat if needed.

1.

Hundreds	Tens	Ones

2.

Hundreds	Tens	Ones

Solve each problem. Use models and your workmat if needed.

3. Model Write the number based on the model shown.

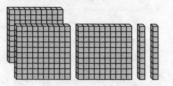

Hundreds	Tens	Ones

4. Number Sense Use the clues to solve the number puzzle.

I have a 5 in my ones place.
The digit in my tens place is 3 plus the digit in my ones place. The digit in my hundreds place is 2 less than the digit in my ones place. What number am I?

_____

5. Higher Order Thinking Look back at Item 4. Write your own place-value number puzzle. Give it to a friend to solve.

_____

_____

_____

6. ☑ **Assessment Practice** Which number is shown?

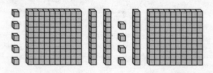

Ⓐ 239

Ⓑ 329

Ⓒ 293

Ⓓ 339

Copyright © Savvas Learning Company LLC. All Rights Reserved.

Additional Practice 9-3
Name Place Values

Another Look! You can find the value of each digit of a number by its place.

Hundreds	Tens	Ones
2	4	3

The value of the 2 is _2 hundreds_ or _200_.

The value of the 4 is _4 tens_ or _40_.

The value of the 3 is _3 ones_ or _3_.

HOME ACTIVITY Choose two three-digit numbers. Ask your child to name the values of each digit in each number.

Use the number in the place-value chart.
Write the value of each digit.

1.

Hundreds	Tens	Ones
8	2	1

The value of the 8 is _____ hundreds or _____.

The value of the 2 is _____ tens or _____.

The value of the 1 is _____ one or _____.

2.

Hundreds	Tens	Ones
5	7	9

The value of the 5 is _____ hundreds or _____.

The value of the 7 is _____ tens or _____.

The value of the 9 is _____ ones or _____.

3. Complete the chart to find the number.

The number has 0 ones.
It has 7 hundreds.
It has 8 tens.

Hundreds	Tens	Ones

What is the number? _____

4. Explain Stacy says the 4 in 643 has a value of 4 tens or 40. Do you agree with Stacy's reasoning? Explain. Use pictures, words, or numbers in your answer.

5. Higher Order Thinking Kayla wrote a three-digit number. The value of the digit in the hundreds place is 6 hundreds. The digit in the tens place is 3 less than the digit in the hundreds place. The sum of all three digits is 12. What is Kayla's number?

Kayla's number is _____.

6. ☑ **Assessment Practice** What is the value of the 7 in the number 763?

Ⓐ 7

Ⓑ 70

Ⓒ 100

Ⓓ 700

Copyright © Savvas Learning Company LLC. All Rights Reserved.

Practice Video Tools Games

Another Look! You can write and show numbers in different ways.

Expanded form uses plus signs to show hundreds, tens, and ones.

$200 + 60 + 4$

You can draw models to show the expanded form.

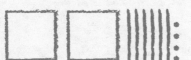

The **word form** is
~~two hundred sixty-four~~.

The **standard form** is
2 6 4 .

HOME ACTIVITY Say a three-digit number, such as eight hundred fifty-one. Write it down in word form. Ask your child to write the number in both standard form and expanded form.

 Solve each problem. Use place-value blocks to help.

1. Draw models to show the expanded form. Write the number in standard form.

$400 + 30 + 8$

four hundred thirty-eight

_____

2. Write the number in expanded form and standard form.

three hundred fifty-four

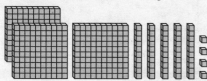

_____ + _____ + _____

_____

3. 🅰🇿 **Vocabulary** Write the number in **standard form**.
Then write it in **word form**.

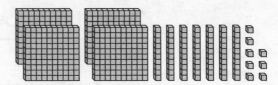

$400 + 70 + 8$

_____

_____

4. ☑ **Assessment Practice** 329 cars and 293 trucks are parked in a parking lot.

Which is the expanded form of the number of cars parked?

Ⓐ $200 + 90 + 3$

Ⓑ $300 + 20 + 9$

Ⓒ $300 + 90 + 2$

Ⓓ $600 + 20 + 2$

Higher Order Thinking Use the clues to complete the number puzzle.

Across

5. $500 + 20 + 3$

7.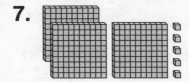

9. $400 + 20 + 9$

10.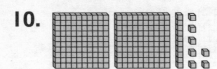

13. Two hundred sixty-nine

Down

6. $300 + 40 + 7$

7. Three hundred ninety-seven

8. $500 + 60 + 9$

11.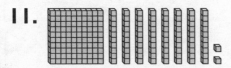

12. Four hundred thirty-eight

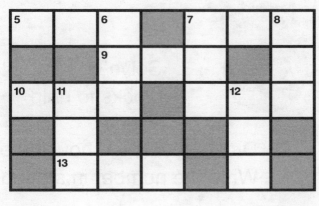

Copyright © Savvas Learning Company LLC. All Rights Reserved.

Topic 9 | Lesson 4

Name _____

Another Look! You can show a number in different ways.

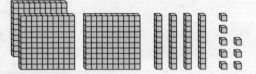

_____3_____ hundreds, ____4____ tens, and ____8____ ones

$348 =$ ___300___ + ___40___ + ___8___ is the same as

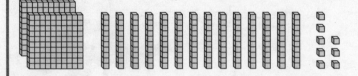

Remember that 10 tens makes 1 hundred. So, 1 hundred and 4 tens is the same as 14 tens.

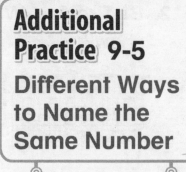

_____2_____ hundreds, ___14___ tens, and ____8____ ones

$348 =$ ___200___ + ___140___ + ___8___

HOME ACTIVITY Write the expanded form of a number and ask your child to tell you another way to show the number. For example, write $200 + 10 + 6$ or $900 + 40 + 3$.

Show two different ways to name the number. You can use place-value blocks to help.

1. $734 =$ _____ hundreds, _____ tens, and _____ ones.

   $734 =$ _____ + _____ + _____

   $734 =$ _____ hundreds, _____ tens, and _____ ones.

   $734 =$ _____ + _____ + _____

2. Be Precise What number does the model show?

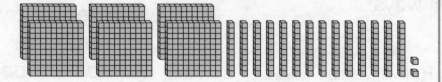

_____

3. Number Sense Write a three-digit number. Then write it in two different ways.

My Number _____

Way 1 _____

Way 2 _____

4. enVision® STEM Matt built a house with 164 blocks. The main part of his house has 100 blocks. The roof has 50 blocks. The chimney has 14 blocks. Write another way to use the same number of blocks for a new house.

Think about place value when you solve this problem.

5. Higher Order Thinking Write 936 two different ways using the charts.

Hundreds	Tens	Ones

Hundreds	Tens	Ones

6. ☑ Assessment Practice Which is a way to show 764? Choose all that apply.

☐ 600 + 150 + 4

☐ 600 + 150 + 14

☐ 700 + 50 + 14

☐ 700 + 60 + 4

 Copyright © Savvas Learning Company LLC. All Rights Reserved.

Practice | Video | Tools | Games

Another Look! The digits in numbers can help you find patterns.

Pick a row in the chart.
Read the numbers across
the row.

975	976	977	978	979	980
985	986	987	988	989	990
995	996	997	998	999	1,000

1,000 comes after 999.

The **ones digits** go up by _____.

Pick a column in the chart and read
the numbers from top to bottom.

The **tens digits** go up by _____.

HOME ACTIVITY Write a three-digit number such as 120. Ask your child to write four more numbers after it, counting by 1s. Then ask your child to start at the number and write four more numbers below it, counting by 10s.

Use place-value patterns and mental math to find the missing numbers.

1.

633		635		637	
	644			647	648
653			656	657	

2.

	285	286			289
294	295		297		299
304			307		

3. Explain Manuel thinks the tens digit goes up by 1 in these numbers. Do you agree? Explain.

460, 470, 480, 490, 500, 510

4. Explain Maribel thinks the tens digit goes up by 1 in these numbers. Do you agree? Explain.

994, 995, 996, 997, 998, 999

5. Higher Order Thinking Write 5 three-digit numbers. From left to right, the ones digit in your numbers should go up by 1.

_____, _____, _____, _____, _____

Write 5 three-digit numbers. From left to right, the tens digit in your numbers should go up by 1.

_____, _____, _____, _____, _____

6. ☑ Assessment Practice Use the numbers on the cards. Write the missing numbers in the number chart.

557 539 545 547

535	536	537	538		540
	546		548	549	550
555	556		558	559	560

Copyright © Savvas Learning Company LLC. All Rights Reserved.

Name _____

Additional Practice 9-7
Skip Count by 5s, 10s, and 100s to 1,000

Another Look! Skip count on the number line. Write the missing numbers.

We are skip counting by 10s!

160, 170, 180, 190...

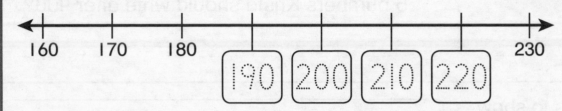

160   170   180 |190| |200| |210| |220| 230

Find the difference between two given numbers that are next to each other. That tells you which number you are skip counting by.

HOME ACTIVITY Draw a number line with numbers that go up by 5s. Have your child tell you what number he or she can skip count by. Repeat this activity with numbers that go up by 10s.

Skip count on the number line. Write the missing numbers.

1.

530   540   550   ☐   ☐   580   ☐   600   ☐   620

2.

100   200   ☐   400   ☐   ☐   ☐   800   ☐   ☐

Solve the problems below.

3. Look for Patterns Bill wants to skip count by 10s from 710. He writes 710, 720, 730 on paper. What are the next 5 numbers Bill should write after 730?

_____, _____, _____, _____, _____

4. Look for Patterns Krista wants to skip count by 100s from 200. She writes 200, 300, 400 on paper. What are the next 5 numbers Krista should write after 400?

_____, _____, _____, _____, _____

5. Higher Order Thinking Linda wants to show skip counting by 5s from a number to get to 1,000. Write the numbers she should put on her number line below. How do you know?

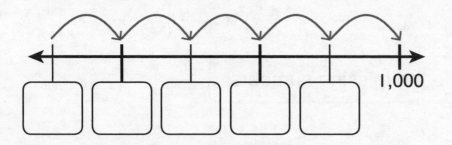

6. ☑ **Assessment Practice** Izzy's family went to a beach 4 times. On their trips, they collected 120, 130, 140, and 150 shells.

Skip counting by what number from 120 to 150 is shown on the number line?

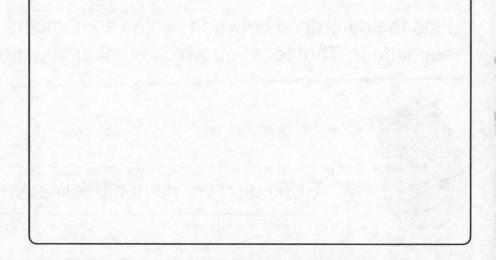

Ⓐ 2   Ⓑ 5   Ⓒ 10   Ⓓ 100

Copyright © Savvas Learning Company LLC. All Rights Reserved.

Name _____

Another Look! To compare two numbers, first compare the digits with the greatest place value.

If the hundreds are equal, compare the tens.
If the tens are equal, compare the ones.

Use models to help!

Hundreds	Tens	Ones
1	1	7
1	1	6

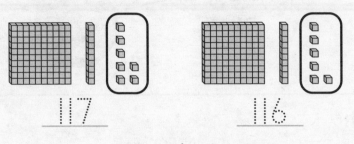

117   116

7 is _greater than_ 6.

So 117 (>) 116.

> means greater than.
< means less than.
= means equals.

HOME ACTIVITY Ask your child if 540 is greater than or less than 524. Then have your child explain his or her answer.

Compare. Write >, <, or =. Use place-value blocks to help if needed.

1. 341 ◯ 432

2. 990 ◯ 290

3. 621 ◯ 639

4. 890 ◯ 880

5. 546 ◯ 546

6. 999 ◯ 995

Make Sense Use the numbers in the triangles as digits. Write a number that will make each comparison true.

7.

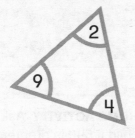

_____ < 942

8.

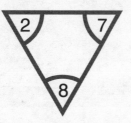

872 > _____

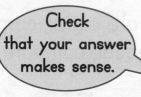

Check that your answer makes sense.

---

9. Nyla compared 790 and 709. Her work is shown at the right.

Is Nyla's comparison correct? If not, correct her mistake.

_____

_____

_____

Nyla's work
790 < 709
I compared the ones.
0 is less than 9.
So, 790 < 709.

---

10. **Higher Order Thinking** A number is less than 200 and greater than 100. The ones digit is 5 less than 10. The tens digit is 2 more than the ones digit. What is the number?

11. ☑ **Assessment Practice** This week, 161 fans watched a soccer game. Last week, 116 fans watched a soccer game. Which correctly compares the number of soccer fans in these two weeks?

Ⓐ 116 = 116   Ⓒ 116 > 161

Ⓑ 161 < 116   Ⓓ 116 < 161

Copyright © Savvas Learning Company LLC. All Rights Reserved.

Name _____

Another Look! Think about the order of numbers.

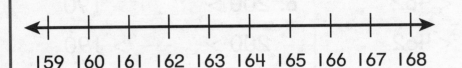

159 160 161 162 163 164 165 166 167 168

Numbers go on forever in both directions on a number line. So, 170 is also greater than 167.

Write a number to make each comparison correct.

__160__ is **less than** 163.   __168__ is **greater than** 167.

__161__ is **greater than** 160 and **less than** 162.

Write a number to make each comparison correct.
Use the number line to help you.

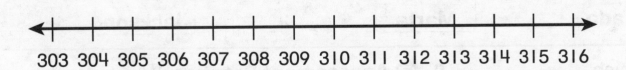

303 304 305 306 307 308 309 310 311 312 313 314 315 316

1. _____ is **less than** 304.

2. _____ is **greater than** 307.

3. _____ is **greater than** 314 and **less than** 316.

HOME ACTIVITY Have your child choose a three-digit number. Then ask your child to name a number that is greater than that number and a number that is less than that number.

Generalize Write three different numbers to make each comparison correct. Draw a number line to help if needed.

4. 805 > _____ > 795

   805 > _____ > 795

   805 > _____ > 795

5. 457 < _____ < 462

   457 < _____ < 462

   457 < _____ < 462

6. 200 > _____ > 190

   200 > _____ > 190

   200 > _____ > 190

7. **Higher Order Thinking** Match each soccer player with a team number. Write the number in the box.

Team Numbers			
192	319	198	420

My number is greater than 197 and less than 199.

My number is less than Carlos's number.

My number is less than 421 and greater than 419.

My number is greater than Carlos's number and less than Marta's number.

Carlos

Jada

Marta

Jackson

8. ☑ **Assessment Practice** Which comparisons are correct? Choose all that apply.

☐ 294 < 293   ☐ 296 > 295

☐ 295 < 298   ☐ 297 = 297

9. ☑ **Assessment Practice** Which number is less than 909 and greater than 868?

Ⓐ 969   Ⓒ 688

Ⓑ 896   Ⓓ 919

Copyright © Savvas Learning Company LLC. All Rights Reserved.

Name _____

Additional Practice 9-10
Look For and Use Structure

Another Look! Sam needs to paint his taxi number on his taxi.

His number is the next greatest number in the pattern.

What is Sam's taxi number?

First sort the numbers from least to greatest.

405 415 410 400 ?

400, 405, 410, 415

Then look for a pattern and name the pattern rule.

The hundreds digit stays the same. The numbers increase by 5 each time.

The pattern rule is increase by 5! Sam's taxi number is 420.

HOME ACTIVITY Write the numbers 285, 265, 255, 275, and 245 on small pieces of paper. Ask your child to sort the numbers from least to greatest. Then ask your child to tell you the pattern rule and to find the next number in the pattern.

Look for a number pattern to solve.

1. James wants to sort the numbers on his teddy bears from greatest to least. After he sorts the numbers, what number would come next?

First sort the numbers from greatest to least.

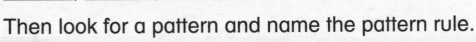
666 676 686 656 ?

_____, _____, _____, _____

Then look for a pattern and name the pattern rule.

_____

What number is next in the pattern? _____

Bicycle Race

Jack and Sara join the purple team for the bike race. Their bike numbers will be the next two greater numbers in the pattern.

Help them find their bike numbers.

2. **Reasoning** List the bike numbers from least to greatest.

_____, _____, _____, _____, _____

3. **Look for Patterns** Look for a pattern and name the pattern rule. What are Jack's and Sara's bike numbers?

_____

_____

_____

4. **Look for Patterns** Suppose new bike numbers are given in decreasing order. Then what numbers would Jack and Sara be given? Explain.

_____

_____

_____

Copyright © Savvas Learning Company LLC. All Rights Reserved.

Practice · Video · Tools · Games

Another Look! Use mental math to add 10 or 100 to 3-digit numbers. Find $315 + 10$ and $315 + 100$.

Place value can help you add 10 or 100 mentally.

HOME ACTIVITY Choose a number between 200 and 300. Ask your child to add 10 to the number and tell you the sum. Repeat with adding 100 to the number.

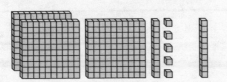

I ten plus I ten is 2 tens.

$315 + 10 = 3\boxed{2}5$

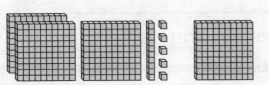

3 hundreds plus I hundred is 4 hundreds.

$315 + 100 = \boxed{4}15$

Add 10 and then add 100 to each number shown. Use blocks if needed.

1.

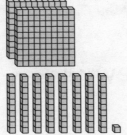

_____ + 10 = _____

_____ + 100 = _____

2.

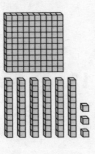

_____ + 10 = _____

_____ + 100 = _____

3.

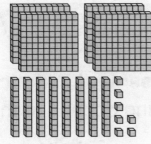

_____ + 10 = _____

_____ + 100 = _____

Look for Patterns Use mental math. Write the missing digit.

4. $100 + \boxed{}00 = 200$

5. $223 + \boxed{}00 = 323$

6. $\$10 + \$351 = \$3\boxed{}1$

🔵 **Vocabulary** Use mental math. Write the missing digit.
Then complete the sentence with **addend** or **sum**.

7. $6\boxed{}3 + 10 = 683$

   683 is the _____.

8. $\boxed{}35 + 100 = 535$

   The _____ is 535.

9. $802 + 10 = 81\boxed{}$

   802 is an _____.

Higher Order Thinking Write the missing digits.

10. $22\boxed{} + 100 + 105 = 4\boxed{}8$

11. $\boxed{}12 + 205 + 10 = 32\boxed{}$

Use mental math to solve.

12. ☑ **Assessment Practice** Which is
the missing addend in the equation?
$\$379 + \underline{\quad} = \$389$

   Ⓐ $10

   Ⓑ $20

   Ⓒ $100

   Ⓓ $380

13. ☑ **Assessment Practice** Which is
the sum of $274 + 100$?

   Ⓐ 174

   Ⓑ 184

   Ⓒ 284

   Ⓓ 374

 Copyright © Savvas Learning Company LLC. All Rights Reserved.

Additional Practice 10-2
Add on an Open Number Line

Another Look! Find 284 + 231.

I can add by 100s, 10s, and 1s or make bigger jumps to find 284 + 231.

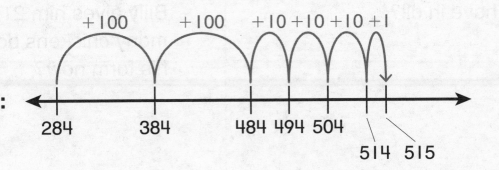

Way 1:

+100   +100   +10 +10 +10 +1

284   384   484 494 504   514 515

HOME ACTIVITY Ask your child to show how he or she would find 153 + 162 using an open number line.

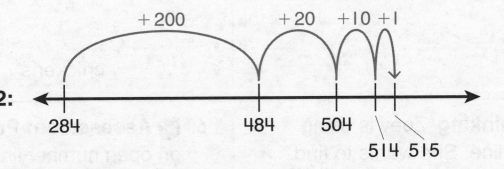

Way 2:

+200   +20 +10 +1

284   484   504   514 515

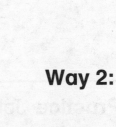

Use an open number line to find each sum.

1. 483 + 172 = _____

2. 288 + 324 = _____

Solve each problem. Use the number line to show your work.

3. Reasoning Jeb has 264 blocks in a box. Mia gives Jeb 341 more blocks. How many blocks does Jeb have in all?

_____ blocks

4. Josh has 509 chickens on his farm. Bob gives Josh 111 chickens, and Billy gives him 21 chickens. How many chickens does Josh have on his farm now?

_____ chickens

5. Higher Order Thinking Zoey is using an open number line. She wants to find 232 + 578. Which addend should she place on the number line to start? Explain.

_____

_____

6. ☑ **Assessment Practice** John uses an open number line to find 570 + 241. One of his jumps is + 40. Draw what John could have done. Write the sum.

$$570 + 241 = \underline{\hspace{2cm}}$$

Copyright © Savvas Learning Company LLC. All Rights Reserved.

Practice   Video   Tools   Games

Additional Practice 10-3
Add Using Models

Another Look! Find 154 + 165.

Step 1: Show each number with place-value blocks.

Hundreds	Tens	Ones

Step 2: Join the hundreds, tens, and ones. Regroup if needed.

Hundreds	Tens	Ones

3 hundreds   **1** ten   **9** ones

So, 154 + 165 = ___319___ .

> Regroup. 10 tens = 1 hundred

HOME ACTIVITY Ask your child to show you how to add 305 + 497 using models. Have your child explain how he or she does the addition.

> Use place-value blocks or drawings to find each sum. Regroup if needed.

1. 248 + 455 = _____

Hundreds	Tens	Ones

2. 209 + 376 = _____

Hundreds	Tens	Ones

3. 594 + 126 = _____

Hundreds	Tens	Ones

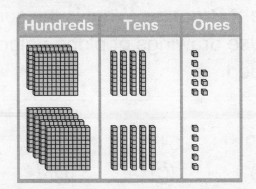

Use place-value blocks or drawings to find each sum. Regroup if needed.

4. 285 + 507 = _____

5. _____ = 378 + 142

6. 371 + 431 = _____

Be Precise Find the total number of buttons for each.
Use the chart. Add using place-value blocks.

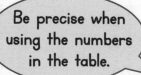

Be precise when using the numbers in the table.

7. Mrs. Jones buys all of the animal and fruit buttons.

8. Mr. Frost buys all of the sport and holiday buttons.

Button	Number
Animal	378
Sport	142
Fruit	296
Holiday	455

7.  _____ ◯ _____ = _____

_____ buttons

8. _____ ◯ _____ = _____

_____ buttons

---

9. Higher Order Thinking A theater manager wants to add 140 seats. Then the theater will have a total of 375 seats. How many seats does the theater have now?

_____ seats

10. ☑ **Assessment Practice** What is the sum of 294 + 225? Use drawings of place-value blocks if needed.

419   509   519   529

Ⓐ   Ⓑ   Ⓒ   Ⓓ

Copyright © Savvas Learning Company LLC. All Rights Reserved.

Topic 10 | Lesson 3

Practice Video Tools Games

Continue to Add Using Models and Place Value

Another Look! Find 135 + 248. Draw blocks for each addend.

Step 1: Join the hundreds. 3 hundreds = 300
Step 2: Join the tens. 7 tens = 70
Step 3: Join the ones. 13 ones = 13
Step 4: Add partial sums.

	Hundreds	Tens	Ones
135	☐	|||	::::
248	☐☐	||||	:::

Add partial sums:
300 + 70 + 13 = 383.

135 + 248 = 383

HOME ACTIVITY Have your child draw place-value blocks and use partial sums to find 158 + 146.

Draw blocks to find the partial sums. Add the partial sums to find the sum.

1. 341 + 127 = _____

	Hundreds	Tens	Ones
	☐☐☐	||||	•
	☐	||	::::

2. 524 + 249 = _____

Hundreds	Tens	Ones

Draw blocks to find the partial sums. Add the partial sums to find the sum.

3. 209 + 123 = _____

Hundreds	Tens	Ones

4. 493 + 265 = _____

Hundreds	Tens	Ones

5. 582 + 356 = _____

Hundreds	Tens	Ones

6. 234 + 427 = _____

Hundreds	Tens	Ones

7. Higher Order Thinking Write and solve an addition story for 482 + 336.

_____

_____

_____

8. ☑ **Assessment Practice** Find 486 + 204. Draw place-value blocks and show partial sums to solve.

486 + 204 = _____

Hundreds	Tens	Ones

Copyright © Savvas Learning Company LLC. All Rights Reserved.

Name _____

Additional Practice 10-5

Add Using Place Value and Partial Sums

Another Look! You can use place value to add two 3-digit numbers.

$164 + 258 = ?$

> Find the partial sums. Then add the partial sums to find the sum.

Hundreds	Tens	Ones

Add the **hundreds**.
Add the **tens**.
Add the **ones**.
Add the partial sums.

Hundreds	Tens	Ones
1	6	4
+ 2	5	8
3	0	0
1	1	0
4	2	2

So, $164 + 258 = \underline{422}$.

HOME ACTIVITY Write $581 + 294$ on a sheet of paper. Ask your child to use partial sums to find the sum.

> Add. Use partial sums. Show your work. Use drawings of blocks if needed.

1. $218 + 136 = ?$

Hundreds	Tens	Ones
2	1	8
+ 1	3	6
Hundreds: 3	0	0
Tens:	4	0
Ones:	1	4
Sum =		

2. $365 + 248 = ?$

Hundreds	Tens	Ones
3	6	5
+ 2	4	8
Hundreds:		
Tens:		
Ones:		
Sum =		

3.   714
    + 135

4.   168
    + 423

5.   266
    + 597

6.   474
    + 238

7.   567
    + 137

8. **Higher Order Thinking** Fill in the missing numbers to make the addition problem true.

	Hundreds	Tens	Ones
	2	☐	8
+	☐	7	☐
Hundreds:	☐	0	0
Tens:		☐	0
Ones:		☐	☐
Sum =	8	9	0

9. ☑ **Assessment Practice** Which is the same amount as 462 + 253? Choose Yes or No.

600 + 11 + 5   ○ Yes ○ No

600 + 110 + 5   ○ Yes ○ No

600 + 100 + 15   ○ Yes ○ No

715   ○ Yes ○ No

There is more than one way to write a sum.

Copyright © Savvas Learning Company LLC. All Rights Reserved.

Practice · Video · Tools · Games

Another Look! Find $219 + 468$.

One Way

You can use mental math and an open number line to keep track of your thinking. Explain your thinking:

I can add numbers in any order.
I can start with 468 and add 219.

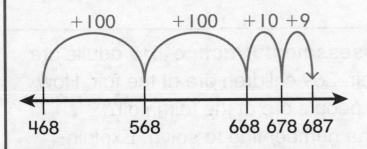

$+100$ $+100$ $+10$ $+9$

468   568   668 678 687

Another Way

You can also use partial sums.

$$\begin{array}{r} 219 \\ + 468 \\ \hline 600 \\ 70 \\ + 17 \\ \hline 687 \end{array}$$

Add partial sums to find the sum.

HOME ACTIVITY Ask your child to choose a strategy to find $429 + 378$. Then have him or her explain why the strategy works.

Choose any strategy to solve each addition problem. Show your work. Then explain your work.

1. $192 + 587 =$ _____

2. $269 + 658 =$ _____

_____

_____

Reasoning Choose any strategy to solve each addition problem. Show your work. Then explain your work.

3. $635 + 284 = $ _____

4. $701 + 103 = $ _____

5. Higher Order Thinking Explain two different ways to find $562 + 399$.

One Way

Another Way

6. ☑ **Assessment Practice** 519 adults are at a fair. 369 children are at the fair. How many people are at the fair in all? Use the number line to solve. Explain.

Copyright © Savvas Learning Company LLC. All Rights Reserved.

Practice   Video   Tools   Games

Another Look! Find 265 + 226.

When you find partial sums, you use repeated reasoning.

I added hundreds first, then tens, and then ones. My sum is 491.

```
  265
+ 226
------
  400
   80
+  11
------
  491
```

I added ones first, then tens, and then hundreds. My sum is also 491.

```
  265
+ 226
------
   11
   80
+ 400
------
  491
```

HOME ACTIVITY Ask your child to solve 204 + 738 using partial sums. Then ask your child to explain how he or she solved the problem.

Use partial sums and repeated reasoning to solve each problem. Show your work. Tell what order you found partial sums in.

1.
```
  244
+ 139
```
_____

_____

_____

2.
```
  371
+ 240
```
_____

_____

_____

Field Trip Costs

Don's class rents a bus for $168. They want to take the bus to the theater. What is the total cost of the bus rental and theater tickets?

Place	Ticket Cost
Science Museum	$158
Horse Farm	$225
Theater	$127

3. Make Sense What do you know? What are you asked to find?

_____

_____

_____

_____

4. Model Write an equation that shows the problem you need to solve.

_____ ◯ _____ = _____

5. Generalize Use what you know about adding 3-digit numbers to solve the problem. Explain what you did.

_____

_____

_____

_____

Copyright © Savvas Learning Company LLC. All Rights Reserved.

Additional Practice 11-1
Subtract 10 and 100

Another Look! Use mental math to subtract 10 or 100 from 3-digit numbers.
Find 278 − 10 and 278 − 100.

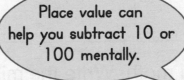

Place value can help you subtract 10 or 100 mentally.

7 tens minus 1 ten

is 6 tens.

278 − 10 = 268

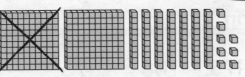

2 hundreds minus 1 hundred

is 1 hundred.

278 − 100 = 178

HOME ACTIVITY Choose a number between 300 and 400. Ask your child to subtract 10 from the number and tell you the difference. Repeat with subtracting 100 from the same number.

Subtract 10 and then subtract 100 from each number shown. Use blocks if needed.

1.

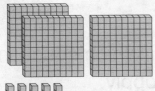

_____ − 10 = _____

_____ − 100 = _____

2.

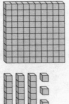

_____ − 10 = _____

_____ − 100 = _____

3.

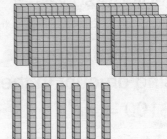

_____ − 10 = _____

_____ − 100 = _____

Look for Patterns Use mental math. Write the missing digit.

4. ☐69 – 100 = 469

5. $☐90 – $100 = $790

6. 402 – 10 = 3☐2

A-Z **Vocabulary** Use mental math. Write the missing digit. Then complete the sentence with **greater than** or **less than**.

7. 271 – 100 = 1☐1

171 is 100 _____ 271.

8. 475 – 100 = ☐75

475 is 100 _____ 375.

9. 612 – ☐0 = 602

602 is ten _____ 612.

---

10. **Higher Order Thinking** Adam is subtracting 708 – 10 mentally. He thinks the tens digit and the hundreds digit will change. He gets 698 for his answer. Is Adam's thinking correct? Explain.

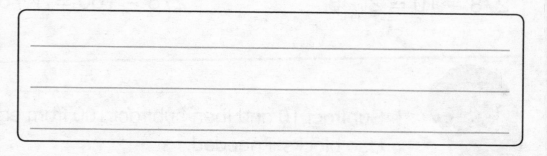

Use mental math to solve.

11. ☑**Assessment Practice** Which is the missing amount in the equation?

$287 – $100 = _____

Ⓐ $387

Ⓒ $187

Ⓑ $277

Ⓓ $87

12. ☑**Assessment Practice** Which equations are true? Choose all that apply.

☐ 144 – 100 = 44

☐ $405 – $10 = $400

☐ 202 – 10 = 192

☐ 560 – 100 = 550

Copyright © Savvas Learning Company LLC. All Rights Reserved.

Name _____

Another Look! Find 664 − 450.

One Way Add Up

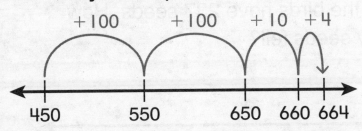

$+100$ $+100$ $+10$ $+4$

450   550   650   660 664

Add hundreds, tens, and ones. $100 + 100 + 10 + 4 = 214$

Another Way Count Back

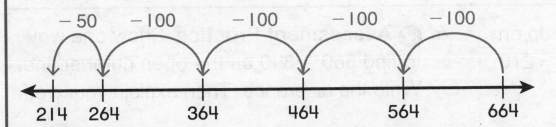

-50 -100 -100 -100 -100

214 264   364   464   564   664

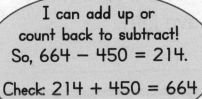

I can add up or count back to subtract! So, 664 − 450 = 214.

Check: 214 + 450 = 664

HOME ACTIVITY Have your child subtract 873 − 659 on an open number line. Then have your child check the answer.

Use the open number line to subtract.

1. 994 − 770 = _____

2. 831 − 716 = _____

Solve each problem. Check your work.

3. Reasoning April has 365 stickers. She gives 238 stickers to Gwen. How many stickers does April have left?

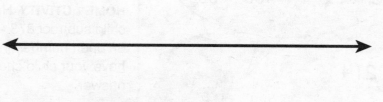

_____ stickers

4. enVision® STEM A group of birds had 362 seeds. Some seeds fell to the ground. Now the birds have 237 seeds. How many seeds fell?

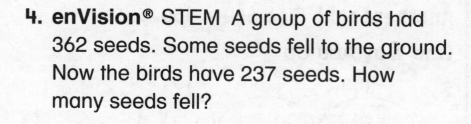

_____ seeds

5. Higher Order Thinking Ricky added up on the number line and found $535 - 315 = 210$. Is his work correct? Explain.

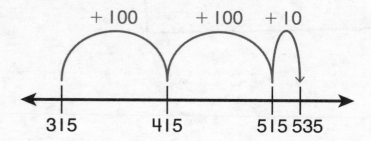

6. ☑ Assessment Practice Show one way to find $560 - 340$ on the open number line. Write the difference. Then explain your work.

$560 - 340 =$ _____

Copyright © Savvas Learning Company LLC. All Rights Reserved.

Practice | Video | Tools | Games

Another Look! You can use drawings to subtract. Find 327 – 164.

One Way
Step 1: Draw 327.
You can subtract the hundreds first.
Subtract 1 hundred.

Hundreds	Tens	Ones

Step 2: Regroup 1 hundred for 10 tens. You can subtract the tens next. Subtract 6 tens. Then subtract the ones. Subtract 4 ones.

Hundreds	Tens	Ones

HOME ACTIVITY Have your child draw place-value blocks to model and find 583 – 274.

So, 327 – 164 = __163__.

Use place-value blocks or drawings to find each difference. Regroup if needed.

1. 549 – 295 = _____

Hundreds	Tens	Ones

2. 835 – 516 = _____

Hundreds	Tens	Ones

Solve the problems below.

3. **Make Sense** Lacy has 517 baseball cards. He has 263 football cards. How many more baseball cards than football cards does he have?

_____ more baseball cards

4. **Higher Order Thinking** Use each number below.

| 8 | 5 | 1 | 8 | 3 | 9 |

Write the subtraction problem that has the greatest difference between two three-digit numbers. Then solve.

_____ – _____ = _____

5. ☑ **Assessment Practice** Which equations are true? Use any strategy to subtract. Choose all that apply.

☐ 825 – 635 = 190

☐ 472 – 129 = 343

☐ 506 – 313 = 193

☐ 999 – 281 = 718

6. ☑ **Assessment Practice** Draw place-value blocks to find 366 – 149. Which is the difference?

Ⓐ 117

Ⓑ 210

Ⓒ 217

Ⓓ 220

Hundreds	Tens	Ones

Copyright © Savvas Learning Company LLC. All Rights Reserved.

Name _____

Another Look! You can use drawings and partial differences to subtract.
Find 361 − 142.

Step 1: Draw 361.
You can subtract the ones first. Subtract 1 of the ones to make a ten.

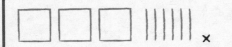 ×

Step 2: Regroup 1 ten for 10 ones. Subtract the other 1. Then subtract the 4 tens and 1 hundred.

Step 3: Record the partial differences.

```
  361
−   1
  360
−   1
  359
−  40
  319
− 100
  219
```

So, 361 − 142 = __219__.

HOME ACTIVITY Ask your child to show you how to subtract 431 − 216. Have your child explain every step of the subtraction.

Draw blocks to find the partial differences. Record the partial differences to find the difference.

1. 412 − 103 = _____

2. 398 − 235 = _____

3. 753 − 304 = _____

Make Sense Mrs. Anderson gives star stickers to her class. She starts with 989 stickers in September. Find out how many she has left as the months go by. Use any strategy. Show your work.

4. In September, Mrs. Anderson gives away 190 stickers.

$989 - 190 = $ _____

_____ stickers

5. In October and November, Mrs. Anderson gives away 586 stickers.

_____ $-$ _____ $=$ _____

_____ stickers

6. In December, Mrs. Anderson gives away 109 more stickers.

_____ $-$ _____ $=$ _____

_____ stickers

---

7. Higher Order Thinking Kelly cuts out 265 strips of paper for an art project. She glues some strips of paper to her piece of art. Now she has 138 strips of paper left. How many strips of paper did Kelly use?

$265 - $ _____ $= 138$

_____ strips of paper

8. ☑ **Assessment Practice** Which numbers complete this partial difference problem for $764 - 372$? Choose all that apply.

```
   764
 - 300
 ─────
     ?
 -   2
 ─────
   462
 -  60
 ─────
   402
 -  10
 ─────
     ?
```

☐ 464   ☐ 402

☐ 462   ☐ 392

Copyright © Savvas Learning Company LLC. All Rights Reserved.

Practice **Video** **Tools** **Games**

Another Look! Find 725 − 592.

One Way Add up to subtract.

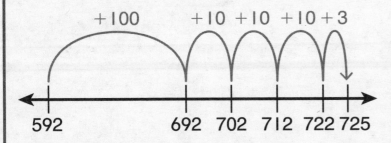

+100   +10 +10 +10 +3

592   692 702 712 722 725

Add hundreds, tens, and ones.

$100 + 10 + 10 + 10 + 3 = 133$

So, $725 − 592 = 133$.

Another Way Add 8 to 592 to make it easy to subtract.

$725 − 600 = 125$

Since you subtracted 8 too many, add 8 to get the difference.

$125 + 8 = 133$

So, $725 − 592 = 133$.

HOME ACTIVITY Ask your child to find 597 − 217 using a subtraction strategy he or she chooses. Then have your child explain why he or she thinks the strategy works.

Choose any strategy to solve each subtraction problem. Show your work. Then explain why the strategy works.

1. $926 − 407 =$ _____

2. $532 − 241 =$ _____

3. Explain Tanner wants to count back on an open number line to find 577 − 479. Marci wants to use mental math to find the difference. Which strategy do you think works better? Why? Show how you would find 577 − 479.

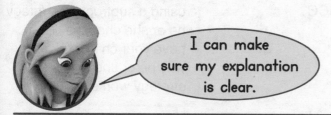

I can make sure my explanation is clear.

4. Higher Order Thinking Danny wants to draw place-value blocks to find 342 − 127. Draw the blocks he would use. Explain why this strategy works.

_____

_____

_____

5. ☑ Assessment Practice Landon counted back on this open number line to find 898 − 133.

Use the numbers on the cards to find the missing numbers in the open number line. Write the missing numbers.

| 778 | 898 | 765 | 798 |

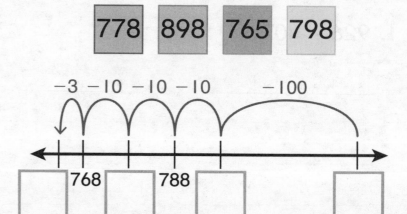

Copyright © Savvas Learning Company LLC. All Rights Reserved.

Practice Video Tools Games

Another Look! You need to use more than one step to solve some problems.

Read the problem. Complete the steps to solve.

Carl has 254 baseball cards.
He gives 145 cards to John and 56 to Amy.
How many cards does Carl have left?

Step 1: Add to find the number of cards Carl gives to John and Amy.

$$145 + 56 = 201$$

Step 2: Subtract the number of cards Carl gives away from the number of cards he has.

$$254 - 201 = 53 \qquad \underline{53} \text{ cards left}$$

HOME ACTIVITY Ask your child to make up a math story that can be solved by adding or subtracting. Then have your child make up a new math story that can be solved using the answer to the first problem.

Think: Is there a hidden question to answer first?

Think: Does my answer make sense?

 Solve the problem. Show your work.
Be ready to explain why your answer makes sense.

1. Mr. Wu buys a box of 300 nails. He uses 156 nails to build a deck. He uses 98 nails to build stairs. How many nails are left?

A School of Fish

Some fish travel in large groups called schools. Swimming in schools helps keep fish safe.

375 fish are swimming in a school. First, 47 fish swim away. Then 116 more fish join the school. How many fish are in the school now?

2. Reasoning Which operations will you use to find how many fish are in the school now? Explain.

_____

_____

_____

3. Generalize Are there now more or less than 375 fish in the school? Explain how you know.

_____

_____

_____

4. Make Sense How many fish are in the school now? Show your work.

Copyright © Savvas Learning Company LLC. All Rights Reserved.

Another Look!

A small paper clip is about 1 inch long.

about 1 inch

A scarf is about 1 yard long. There are 3 feet in 1 yard.

about 1 yard

A tablet computer is about 1 foot long. There are 12 inches in 1 foot.

about 1 foot

HOME ACTIVITY Have your child identify three objects that are about 1 inch, 1 foot, and 1 yard in length or height.

About how long or tall is each object? Circle the answer.

1.    about 1 inch

about 1 foot

about 1 yard

2. 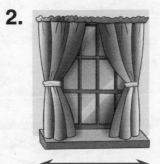   about 1 inch

about 1 foot

about 1 yard

3.    about 1 inch

about 1 foot

about 1 yard

Reasoning Choose three objects and estimate their length or height in inches, feet, or yards. Draw a picture and write the name of each object. Write the estimated length or height next to each object.

4.

5.

6.

---

7. Higher Order Thinking Mia has 4 tiles. Jake has 5 tiles. Each tile is about 1 inch long. They use all of their tiles to measure the height of this water bottle. What is the estimated height of the water bottle?

About _____ inches

8. ☑ **Assessment Practice** Draw a line from each estimate to a matching object.

| About 1 inch | About 1 foot | About 1 yard |

Copyright © Savvas Learning Company LLC. All Rights Reserved.

Topic 12 | Lesson 1

Name _____

Another Look! You can use a ruler to measure inches.

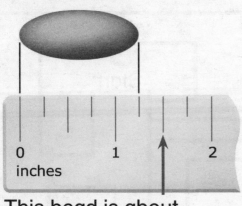

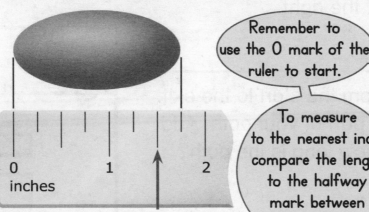

Remember to use the 0 mark of the ruler to start.

To measure to the nearest inch, compare the length to the halfway mark between inches.

0 inches   1   2

0 inches   1   2

This bead is about
_1_ inch long.

This bead is about
_2_ inches long.

HOME ACTIVITY Ask your child to find items at home that are about 1 inch, about 6 inches, and about 12 inches long.

Estimate the height or length of each real object. Then use a ruler to measure. Compare your estimate and measurement.

1. height of a book

My Favorite Book

2. length of a pencil

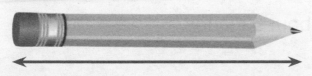

Estimate	Measure
about ___ inches	about ___ inches
about ___ inches	about ___ inches

Solve each problem.

3. Number Sense Estimate how long the path is to get out of the maze shown at the right.

about _____ inches

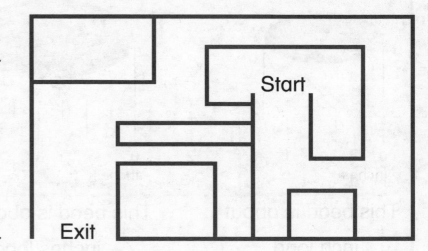

4. Make Sense Draw a path from the start to the exit. Use a ruler to measure each part of your path. Add the lengths together. About how long is the path?

about _____ inches

5. How close to the answer was your estimate?

_____

6. Higher Order Thinking Gina says this straw is about 2 inches long. Sal says it is about 3 inches long. Who is correct? Explain.

_____

_____

_____

7. ☑ Assessment Practice Use a ruler. Measure the length of the pencil in inches. Which is the correct measurement?

Ⓐ about 2 inches

Ⓑ about 3 inches

Ⓒ about 4 inches

Ⓓ about 5 inches

 Copyright © Savvas Learning Company LLC. All Rights Reserved. **Topic 12** | Lesson 2

Name _____

Another Look! You can use a yardstick to measure objects to the nearest foot.

Remember, I foot is 12 inches long.
So, 2 feet are 24 inches long.
I yard is 36 inches long
or 3 feet long.

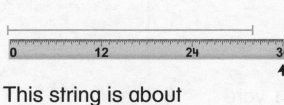
Think: Is the string closer to 2 feet long or closer to 3 feet long?

HOME ACTIVITY Have your child identify three objects at home that are about I inch, I foot, and I yard in length.

This string is about
__2__ feet long.

This string is about
__3__ feet long.

Estimate the height or length of each object. Then measure to the nearest unit.

I. The height of the doorway

Estimate: about _____ feet

Measure: about _____ feet

2. The height of a chair

Estimate: about _____ inches

Measure: about _____ inches

3. The width of a window

Estimate: about _____ yards

Measure: about _____ yards

Solve each problem. Show your work.

4. Reasoning Draw a picture of and name objects that have these lengths.

More than 6 inches but less than 1 foot

More than 1 foot but less than 2 feet

More than 2 feet but less than 1 yard

5. enVision® STEM Jay planted sunflowers in a sunny spot. He gave them water and watched them grow to be taller than he is. He measured the heights of the plants when they were full-grown. Were they 8 inches or 8 feet tall? Explain.

_____

_____

_____

_____

6. Higher Order Thinking Which tool would you choose to measure the number of inches around your waist? Explain.

_____

_____

_____

7. ☑ Assessment Practice Use a ruler. About how long is the crayon?

Ⓐ about 1 inch

Ⓑ about 2 inches

Ⓒ about 4 inches

Ⓓ about 6 inches

Copyright © Savvas Learning Company LLC. All Rights Reserved.

Name _____

Practice Video Tools Games

Additional
Practice 12-4
Measure Length
Using Different
Customary Units

Another Look! You can measure using different units.

Derrick measured the gift box in inches and in feet.

The gift box is about
___ inches long.

The gift box is about
___ foot long.

It takes more units of inches than feet to measure the gift box because an inch is a smaller unit.

If you use smaller units, you need to use more units.

HOME ACTIVITY Have your child use a foot ruler to measure objects in both inches and in feet. Then ask your child if he or she used more units of inches or feet to measure each object.

Measure each object using different units.
Circle the unit you use *more* of to measure each object.

1.

about _____ feet   about _____ yards

I use more units of: feet   yards

2.

about _____ inches   about _____ feet

I use more units of: inches   feet

Solve each problem.

3. Explain Trina says that her dollhouse is about 8 yards tall. Is Trina's estimate a good estimate? Explain.

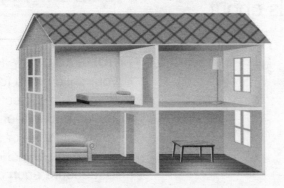

_____

_____

4. Higher Order Thinking Will it take fewer foot-long rulers or fewer yardsticks to measure the length of a real car? Explain.

_____

_____

5. ☑ Assessment Practice Which unit would you need the most of to measure the height of the umbrella?

Ⓐ inches

Ⓑ feet

Ⓒ yards

Ⓓ all the same

6. ☑ Assessment Practice Which is the best estimate for the length of a pen?

Ⓐ about 10 inches

Ⓑ about 6 inches

Ⓒ about 5 feet

Ⓓ about 10 yards

Copyright © Savvas Learning Company LLC. All Rights Reserved.

Name _____

Another Look! You can use a ruler to measure centimeters.

To measure to the nearest centimeter, look at the halfway mark between centimeters. If the object is longer, use the greater number. If the object is shorter, use the smaller number.

HOME ACTIVITY Ask your child to find items at home that measure about 1 centimeter, about 10 centimeters, and about 100 centimeters. If possible, use a ruler to measure each object.

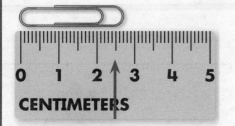

The paper clip is about
3 centimeters long.

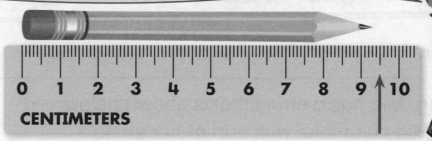

This pencil is about
9 centimeters long.

Estimate the height or length of each real object. Then use a ruler to measure. Compare your estimate and measurement.

1. length of a tape dispenser

2. height of a book

	Estimate	Measure
1.	about ____ centimeters	about ____ centimeters
2.	about ____ centimeters	about ____ centimeters

Solve each problem.

3. **Use Tools** Measure the length of this spoon in centimeters.
About how long is the spoon?

About _____ centimeters   What tool did you use? _____

4. **Higher Order Thinking** Mia has a string that is shown below.
Circle the shapes that Mia can make with part of her string.

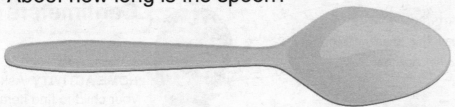

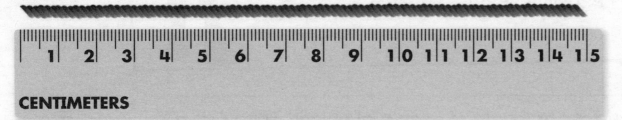

1 2 3 4 5 6 7 8 9 10 11 12 13 14 15

CENTIMETERS

Use the measurements given on the shapes to decide.

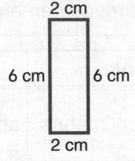
3 cm 5 cm 4 cm

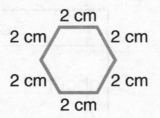
2 cm 6 cm 6 cm 2 cm

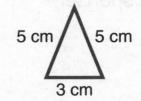
2 cm 2 cm 2 cm 2 cm 2 cm 2 cm

5 cm 5 cm 3 cm

3 cm 3 cm 3 cm 3 cm

5. ✓ **Assessment Practice** Measure this paper clip. How many centimeters long is the paper clip?

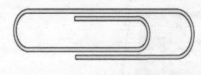

_____ centimeters

Copyright © Savvas Learning Company LLC. All Rights Reserved.

Name _____

Another Look! You can use a meter stick to measure length in meters.

Step 1: Line up a meter stick with one end of an object.

Step 2: Mark the spot where the other end of the meter stick sits on the object.

Step 3: Then move the meter stick so the 0 end starts where you marked.

You can also measure the length in centimeters.

The table is about 2 meters long.

HOME ACTIVITY Have your child show you an object at home that is about a centimeter long and another object that is about a meter long.

Estimate the height or length of each real object. Then measure. Compare your estimate and measurement.

1. The length of a table

   Estimate:

   about _____ meters

   Measure:

   about _____ meters

2. The height of a chair

   Estimate:

   about _____ centimeters

   Measure:

   about _____ centimeters

3. The length of your room

   Estimate:

   about _____ meters

   Measure:

   about _____ meters

4. enVision® STEM Sarah put bean plants by a window with sunlight. She watered them every other day. Sarah measured the height of the plants after 3 weeks. Do you think they measured 12 centimeters or 12 meters? Explain.

_____

_____

_____

5. Reasoning What would be a reasonable estimate for the length of a calculator?

about _____ centimeters

6. Higher Order Thinking Do you need fewer units of centimeters or meters to measure the height of a doorway? Explain.

_____

_____

_____

_____

7. ☑ Assessment Practice Which measures are reasonable estimates for the length of a bedroom? Choose all that apply.

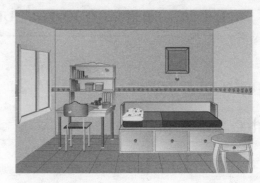

☐ 4 centimeters   ☐ 3 meters

☐ 4 meters   ☐ 30 centimeters

    Copyright © Savvas Learning Company LLC. All Rights Reserved.

Practice Video Tools Games

Another Look! You can measure using different units.

Andy measures the length of the television using both centimeters and meters.

The television is about

_1_ meter long.

The television is about

_88_ centimeters long.

It takes fewer units of meters than centimeters to measure the television.
If you use larger units, you will use fewer of them.

HOME ACTIVITY Select two objects in your home, such as a table or a window. Ask your child if he or she would use more units of centimeters or meters to measure each object.

Measure each object using centimeters and meters.
Circle the unit you use *fewer* of to measure each object.

1.

about _____ centimeters   about _____ meters

I use fewer units of: centimeters   meters

2.

about _____ centimeters   about _____ meters

I use fewer units of: centimeters   meters

Solve each problem.

3. **Make Sense** Circle the objects that are easier to measure using centimeters. Cross out the objects that are easier to measure using meters.

4. **Higher Order Thinking** Shane and Karen want to measure the length of a soccer field.
Should they use centimeters or meters to measure it? Explain.

_____

_____

_____

Think about the size of one unit.

5. ☑ **Assessment Practice** Carlos measures the length of a couch in centimeters and meters. How will his measurements compare?

Choose Yes or No.

More units of centimeters than meters	○ Yes	○ No
Fewer units of meters than centimeters	○ Yes	○ No
Equal number of units of centimeters and meters	○ Yes	○ No

Copyright © Savvas Learning Company LLC. All Rights Reserved.
Topic 12 | Lesson 7

Practice Video Tools Games

Another Look! You can write an equation to help you find the total length of a path. What is the total length of Path A?

Path A

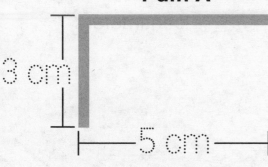

3 cm

5 cm

3 + 5 = 8

Measure each part of a path to start.

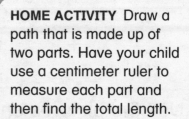

Path A is about ___8___ centimeters long.

HOME ACTIVITY Draw a path that is made up of two parts. Have your child use a centimeter ruler to measure each part and then find the total length.

Use a centimeter ruler to measure Path B. Answer each question.

1. **Path B**

____ + ____ = ____

about ____ centimeters long

2. Which path is longer, Path A or Path B?

Path A

Path B

3. How much longer is the longer path than the shorter path?

about ____ centimeter longer

Solve each problem.

4. Model Joanna drew a path that is 8 cm shorter than Liam's path. Joanna's path is 19 cm long. How long is Liam's path? Write an equation.

_____ + _____ = _____ centimeters

5. Model Nadine drew a path that is 7 cm longer than Nancy's path. Nadine's path is 15 cm long. How long is Nancy's path? Write an equation.

_____ – _____ = _____ centimeters

Use the pictures on the right to solve each problem.

6. Kristin cleans out her desk. Write the items she finds in order from longest to shortest. Then fill in the blanks for each sentence below.

_____   _____   _____

Longest   Shortest

7. Higher Order Thinking Fill in the missing words.

The pencil is _____ than the ruler,

and the ruler is shorter than the

_____. So, the pencil is

_____ than the _____ .

8. ☑ **Assessment Practice** Use a centimeter ruler. How much longer is the black path than the gray path?

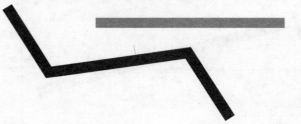

Ⓐ about 2 cm   Ⓒ about 4 cm

Ⓑ about 3 cm   Ⓓ about 5 cm

Copyright © Savvas Learning Company LLC. All Rights Reserved.

Name _____

Practice   Video   Tools   Games

Another Look! Amy uses a button to measure the length of a glue stick. One button is 1 centimeter tall. She finds that the glue stick is 5 cm long.

Amy used a ruler to check her work. She started at the 0 mark.

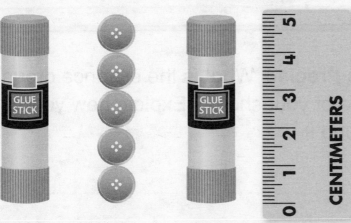

First time: 5 cm   Second time: 5 cm

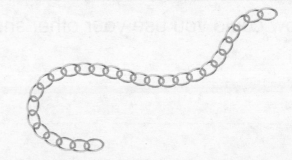

Amy got the same answer both times. So, she knows her work is precise! It helps to measure twice!

HOME ACTIVITY Have your child measure the length of a household item. Have your child choose the unit to use. Ask your child to explain how he or she knows the measurement is precise.

Solve the problem. You can use string or buttons to help.

1. Find the length of the chain at the right.
   Estimate and use tools to measure.

   Estimate: _____

   Actual measurement: _____

Distance Around Your Shoe

Shoes have different sizes and shapes.
The picture shows the bottom of a shoe.
What is the total distance around the bottom
of one of your shoes?

2. **Reasoning** What units of measure will you use? Explain.

_____

_____

_____

_____

3. **Be Precise** What is the distance around one of your shoes? Explain how you found it.

_____

_____

_____

_____

_____

4. **Explain** How could you use your other shoe to check your work?

_____

_____

 Copyright © Savvas Learning Company LLC. All Rights Reserved. **Topic 12** | Lesson 9

Name _____

Another Look! You can name shapes by their number of sides and vertices.

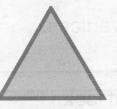 A triangle has

_3_ sides and

_3_ vertices.

 A quadrilateral has

_4_ sides and

_4_ vertices.

 A pentagon has

_5_ sides and

_5_ vertices.

 A hexagon has

_6_ sides and

_6_ vertices.

HOME ACTIVITY Look around your home for items that are shaped like triangles, quadrilaterals, pentagons, or hexagons. Ask your child to tell the number of sides and vertices for each shape.

Name each shape.
Write the number of sides and vertices.

1.

Shape: _____

____ sides

____ vertices

2.

Shape: _____

____ sides

____ vertices

3.

Shape: _____

____ sides

____ vertices

4. Algebra Leona drew 2 pentagons.

She drew _____ vertices.

5. Algebra Nestor drew 3 quadrilaterals.

He drew _____ sides.

6. Algebra Kip drew a hexagon and a triangle.

He drew _____ vertices.

7. Model Draw 2 hexagons that look different from the one shown.

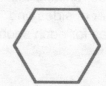

8. Model Draw 2 quadrilaterals that look different from the one shown.

9. Higher Order Thinking Tami traced the flat sides of this block.
What shapes did she draw?
Name and draw the shapes.

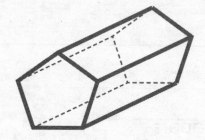

10. ☑ **Assessment Practice** Jin drew two shapes. One of the shapes is shown below.
If Jin drew 9 sides and 9 vertices in all, which other shape did he draw?

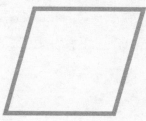

Ⓐ triangle   Ⓒ rectangle

Ⓑ rhombus   Ⓓ pentagon

Copyright © Savvas Learning Company LLC. All Rights Reserved.

Practice Video Tools Games

Additional Practice 13-2
Polygons and Angles

Another Look! Polygons are closed plane shapes with 3 or more sides. Polygons have the same number of angles and vertices as sides.

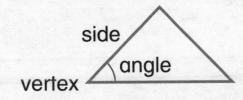
side
angle
vertex

Name and describe this polygon.

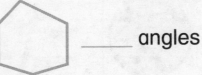

An angle that forms a square corner is called a right angle.

HOME ACTIVITY Ask your child to find objects that have polygon shapes. Have your child name each shape and tell how many angles it has.

Pentagon 5 sides 5 vertices 5 angles

Write the number of angles and then name the shape.

1. _____ angles

Shape: _____

2. _____ angles

Shape: _____

3. _____ angles

Shape: _____

4. Be Precise The sign below tells drivers to yield. This means to wait for other cars or people to go first.
Which polygon shape do you see in the sign?

5. (A-Z) **Vocabulary** The outside edges of this nut for a bolt form a **polygon** shape. Name that shape.

6. Higher Order Thinking Look at the design below. Write three names for the shape that has right angles.

Remember! A right angle forms a square corner.

7. ☑ **Assessment Practice** Name the shape below. Write 3 things that describe the shape.

Copyright © Savvas Learning Company LLC. All Rights Reserved.

Another Look! The number of sides in a polygon is the same as the number of vertices and the number of angles.

Draw a polygon with 6 vertices.

The sides can be the same length.   The sides can be different lengths.

Each polygon has ___6___ vertices.

Each polygon also has ___6___ sides and ___6___ angles.

Both polygons are ___hexagons___ .

What pattern do you see?

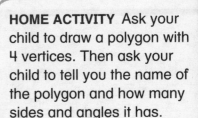

HOME ACTIVITY Ask your child to draw a polygon with 4 vertices. Then ask your child to tell you the name of the polygon and how many sides and angles it has.

Draw two different polygons for each number of vertices.

1. 4 vertices

Each polygon has _____ sides.

Both polygons are _____.

2. 5 vertices

Each polygon has _____ angles.

Both polygons are _____.

Draw each polygon. Then complete the sentences.

3. It has 2 fewer sides than a pentagon.

The shape is a _____.

4. It has 3 more vertices than a triangle.

The shape is a _____.

5. Make Sense It has I less vertex than a hexagon and 2 more angles than a triangle.

The shape is a _____.

6. Higher Order Thinking Tanika has 7 toothpicks. She uses them all to create two polygons. Draw two polygons that Tanika could have created. Write the names of your shapes.

7. ☑ **Assessment Practice** Kit drew a polygon that has 4 vertices. Which could **NOT** be Kit's polygon?

Ⓐ quadrilateral

Ⓑ triangle

Ⓒ rectangle

Ⓓ square

8. ☑ **Assessment Practice** Reg drew a polygon with more sides than a square and fewer vertices than a hexagon. Which could Reg have drawn?

Ⓐ triangle

Ⓑ rectangle

Ⓒ quadrilateral

Ⓓ pentagon

Copyright © Savvas Learning Company LLC. All Rights Reserved.

Name _____

Another Look! You can tell if a shape is a cube by counting its faces, vertices, and edges. Number cubes are examples of real-life objects that are cubes.

Every cube has 6 equal square faces, 8 vertices, and 12 edges.

These real-life objects are **NOT** cubes.

  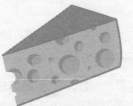

HOME ACTIVITY Have your child find an object at home that has a cube shape. Ask your child to describe the object including the number of faces, vertices, and edges.

Tell whether each shape or object is a cube. If it is not a cube, tell what shape it is. Then explain how you know.

1.  _____

_____

_____

_____

2. _____

_____

_____

_____

Use what you know about cubes to solve each problem.

3. **Look for Patterns** You can make two squares to draw a cube.

1. Connect the 4 black dots to make one square.

2. Connect the 4 gray dots to make another square.

3. Connect each corner of the black square to a like corner of the gray square.

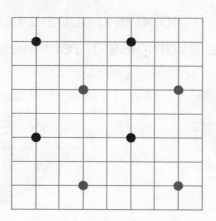

> This is another way to draw a cube.

4. **Higher Order Thinking** Look at the solid figure below. Count the number of faces, vertices, and edges it has. Why is this figure **NOT** a cube?

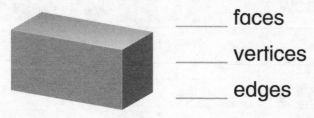

_____ faces

_____ vertices

_____ edges

_____

_____

5. ☑ **Assessment Practice** Circle the shapes that are **NOT** cubes. Explain how you know.

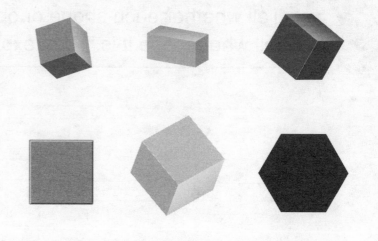

_____

Copyright © Savvas Learning Company LLC. All Rights Reserved.

Another Look! How many squares cover this rectangle?

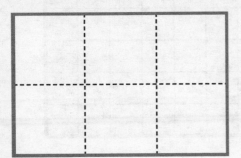

You can use square tiles to cover rectangles. Count the squares in the rows. Then count the squares in the columns.

HOME ACTIVITY Ask your child to draw a rectangular section of a floor made of square tiles. Then ask your child to count how many squares make up that rectangle.

Add the rows: $3 + 3 = 6$

Add the columns: $2 + 2 + 2 = 6$

Use square tiles to cover the rectangle. Trace the tiles. Count the squares.

1.

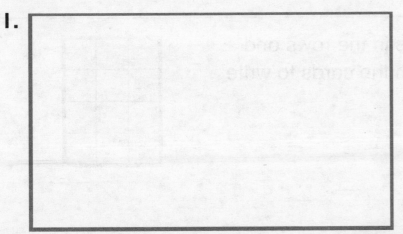

2. How many squares cover the rectangle?

Add by rows:

____ + ____ + ____ = ____

Add by columns:

____ + ____ + ____ + ____ + ____

= ____

Solve each problem.

3. **Look for Patterns** Mr. Cory puts square tiles on the kitchen floor. The square tiles are all the same size. How many equal squares are there? Write two equations to show the total number of square tiles.

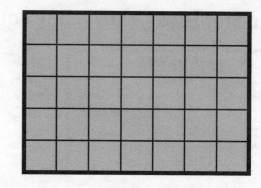

Rows:

_____ + _____ + _____ + _____ + _____ = _____ tiles

Columns:

_____ + _____ + _____ + _____ + _____ + _____ + _____ = _____ tiles

4. **Higher Order Thinking** 10 friends want to equally share a rectangular pan of granola bars. Show the rectangle in 10 equal pieces.

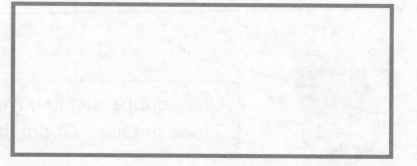

5. ☑ **Assessment Practice** Count the equal squares in the rows and columns of the rectangle. Then use the numbers on the cards to write the missing numbers in the equations.

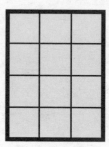

| 4 | 12 | 3 |

Rows: _____ + _____ + _____ + _____ = _____

Columns: _____ + _____ + _____ = _____

Copyright © Savvas Learning Company LLC. All Rights Reserved.

Name _____

Another Look! Equal shares are the same size.

2 equal shares	3 equal shares	4 equal shares
 (halves) thirds fourths	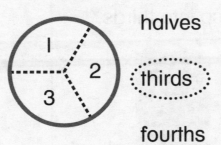 halves (thirds) fourths	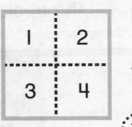 halves thirds (fourths)

HOME ACTIVITY Draw three squares. Ask your child to draw lines in one square to show halves. Then have your child draw lines in the second square to show thirds, and draw lines in the third square to show fourths.

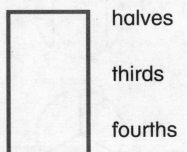 Draw the number of equal shares given for each shape. Then circle the word that describes the shares.

1. 4 equal shares

halves

thirds

fourths

2. 3 equal shares

halves

thirds

fourths

3. 2 equal shares

halves

thirds

fourths

4. 4 equal shares

halves

thirds

fourths

 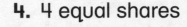

5. Two students want to equally share a small pizza. Draw how to split the pizza into halves.

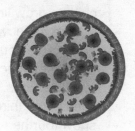

6. Three students want to equally share a tray of apple crisp. Draw two ways to split the apple crisp into thirds.

7. Four students want to share an apple pie. Draw lines to split the pie into fourths.

8. Higher Order Thinking This shape is shown with four pieces. Ryan says this shape is shown in fourths. Is he correct? Explain.

_____

_____

9. ☑ **Assessment Practice** Tom cut his muffin in half to share it with his brother. Which pictures do **NOT** show halves? Choose all that apply.

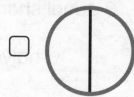 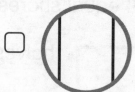

Copyright © Savvas Learning Company LLC. All Rights Reserved.

Name _____

Practice   Video   Tools   Games

Another Look!

You can show a rectangle with equal shares in different ways.

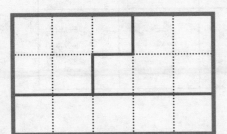   

Each equal share has 5 squares.

Each rectangle has 3 equal shares. Each equal share has 5 squares.

HOME ACTIVITY Draw a rectangle. Ask your child to show it with two equal shares that have different shapes.

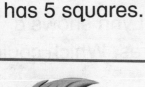

Draw lines to show three different ways to show 2 equal shares.

1.

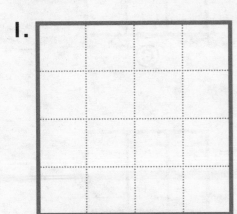   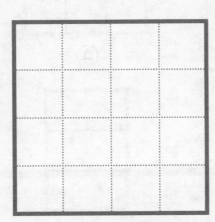   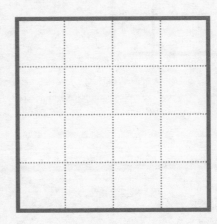

Can you show a rectangle with equal shares that have DIFFERENT shapes?

Solve each problem.

2. Explain Lexi wants to share the sheet of tiger stickers with two friends. Are there enough stickers to make equal shares for Lexi and her two friends? Explain.

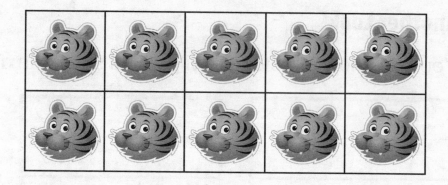

_____

_____

_____

3. Higher Order Thinking Corbin drew the dark lines inside this rectangle to make equal shares. Did he make equal shares? Explain.

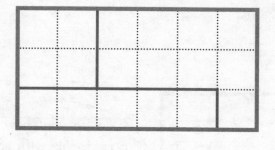

_____

_____

_____

4. **Assessment Practice** Lynn shows a rectangle with 3 equal shares. Which could **NOT** be Lynn's rectangle?

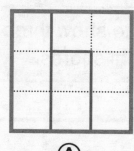

Ⓐ

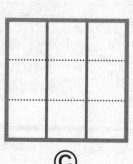

Ⓒ

Ⓑ

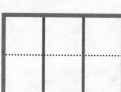

Ⓓ

Copyright © Savvas Learning Company LLC. All Rights Reserved.

Name _____

Another Look! Create two different designs for these squares that are the same size. Each design needs to have 2 colors with an equal share for each color.

I can draw a line down the center to make equal shares.

I can draw a line from opposite corners to make equal shares.

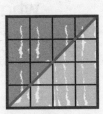

Design 1

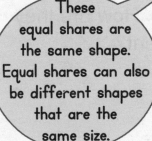

Design 2

These equal shares are the same shape. Equal shares can also be different shapes that are the same size.

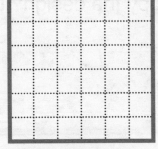

HOME ACTIVITY Draw two identical rectangles. Have your child use crayons to draw a different design in each rectangle. Each rectangle should show 4 equal shares, each in a different color.

Solve the problem. Use crayons to color. Explain your solution.

1. Make two different designs. Each design must have 3 colors with an equal share for each color. One design should have shares that are NOT all the same shape.

_____

_____

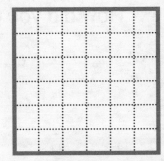

Design 1   **Design 2**

A Design Repeated

Steven created this design on 4 squares of grid paper.
He wants to repeat this design 6 times on a larger grid.
Answer the questions to help Steven create the larger design.

2. **Look for Patterns** Look at each small square of Steven's design. How are they alike? How are they different?

_____

_____

_____

3. **Explain** Describe Steven's design. Explain what it looks like. Use *half of*, *a third of*, or *a fourth of* when you describe it.

_____

_____

_____

4. **Generalize** Copy Steven's design 4 times.
Use 2 colors. Put 2 designs next to each other in each row.

How did you copy the design? Describe a shortcut you used.

_____

_____

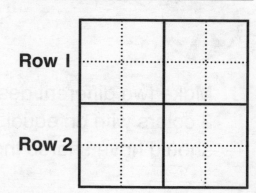

Row 1

Row 2

Copyright © Savvas Learning Company LLC. All Rights Reserved.

Name _____

Another Look!

You can use addition or subtraction to solve problems with measurements. How much longer is the snake than the worm?

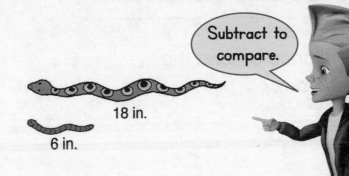

Subtract to compare.

18 in.

6 in.

$$18 - 6 = 12$$

The snake is __12 inches__ longer than the worm.

HOME ACTIVITY Ask your child to find a rectangular object (a book, piece of paper, tile, etc.). Have your child measure each side in inches and write an equation to find the distance around the object.

Decide if you need to add or subtract.
Then write an equation to help solve each problem.

1. How much shorter is the feather than the ribbon?

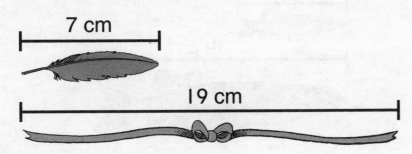

7 cm

19 cm

_____ centimeters shorter

2. What is the distance around the rug?

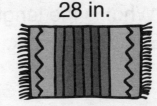

28 in.

15 in.

_____

_____ inches

Decide if you need to add or subtract.
Then write an equation to help solve each problem.

3. **Model** What is the distance around the
front cover of the game box?

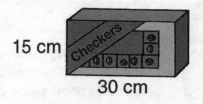

15 cm

30 cm

The distance around the front cover of

the game box is _____ .

You can model a
problem with an equation.
Include the units in
your answer.

4. **Higher Order Thinking** The distance
around Tim's rectangular book is
48 centimeters. The length of each longer
side is 14 cm. What is the length of each
shorter side? Show your work.

Each shorter side of the book is

_____ long.

5. ☑ **Assessment Practice** How much
longer is the bottom fish than the top fish?

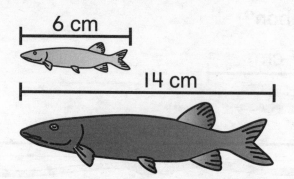

6 cm

14 cm

Ⓐ 7 cm   Ⓒ 20 cm

Ⓑ 8 cm   Ⓓ 40 cm

Copyright © Savvas Learning Company LLC. All Rights Reserved.

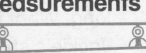

Practice Video Tools Games

Another Look!

Lance's boat is 13 meters long.

Cory's boat is 7 meters longer.

How long is Cory's boat?

You can follow these steps to solve word problems.

You can draw a picture to help.

Step 1 Write an equation to show the problem. $13 + 7 = ?$

Step 2 Draw a picture to help solve.

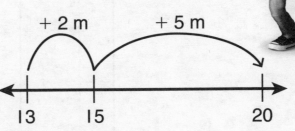

+ 2 m   + 5 m

13   15   20

Step 3 Solve the problem. Cory's boat is 20 meters long.

HOME ACTIVITY Have your child draw a picture to solve this problem. *A building is 24 meters tall. The tree next to the building is 5 meters tall. How much shorter is the tree than the building?*

Write an equation using a ? for the unknown number.
Solve with a picture or another way.

1. Suzy's ribbon is 83 centimeters long.
   She cuts off 15 centimeters. How long is
   Suzy's ribbon now?

   _____   _____ cm

Solve each problem. Show your work.

2. **Make Sense** Jackie's shoelaces are 13 inches, 29 inches, and 58 inches long. What is the total length of all of Jackie's shoelaces? Draw a picture and write an equation to solve.

_____ in.

3. Mary is 2 inches taller than Bill. Bill is 48 inches tall. How tall is Mary?

4. **Higher Order Thinking** Kyle's bedroom is 11 feet long. Garrett's bedroom is 2 feet longer than Kyle's room. Priya's bedroom is 3 feet shorter than Garrett's room. What is the sum of the lengths of Garrett and Priya's bedrooms?

_____ ft

5. ☑ **Assessment Practice** Ryan's desk is 25 inches tall. His floor lamp is 54 inches tall. How many inches taller is Ryan's floor lamp? Write an equation and draw a picture to solve.

_____ inches taller

Copyright © Savvas Learning Company LLC. All Rights Reserved.

Name _____

Another Look!

Kelsey is 59 inches tall.
She grows and is now 73 inches tall.
How many inches did Kelsey grow?

Show the problem with an equation: 59 + ? = 73.

You can draw a picture of a tape measure to solve the problem.

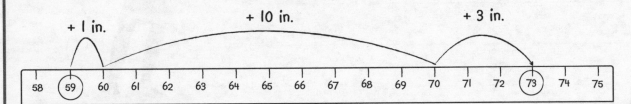

+ 1 in.   + 10 in.   + 3 in.

58 (59) 60 61 62 63 64 65 66 67 68 69 70 71 72 (73) 74 75

Kelsey grew 14 inches.

HOME ACTIVITY Have your child draw a picture and write an equation to solve this problem. *Paul has 45 feet of string. Sal cuts some string off. Now Paul has 38 feet of string. How many feet of string did Sal cut off?*

Write an equation using a ? for the unknown number. Solve with a picture or another way.

1. Brigit has a piece of rope. She ties 18 more meters of rope to her rope. Now the rope is 27 meters long. How long was the rope to begin with?

Solve each problem.

Remember to use the correct words and symbols to explain your thinking.

2. **Explain** Elizabeth ran 36 meters.
Haruki ran 8 fewer meters than Elizabeth.
Delilah ran 3 fewer meters than Haruki.
How many meters did Delilah run?
Explain your thinking.

_____

_____

_____

3. **Higher Order Thinking** The lengths of the pencils are given at the right.

Write and solve a two-step problem about the pencils.

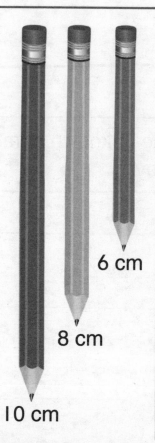

6 cm

8 cm

10 cm

_____

_____

_____

4. ☑ **Assessment Practice** A hammer is 1 foot long. A car is 15 feet long. A shovel is 4 feet long.

Which statements are correct? Choose all that apply.

☐ The car is 9 ft longer than the hammer.

☐ The hammer is 14 ft shorter than the car.

☐ The shovel is 3 ft longer than the hammer.

☐ The car is 11 feet longer than the shovel.

Copyright © Savvas Learning Company LLC. All Rights Reserved.

Name _____

Another Look!

Start at 0. Draw an arrow to show the first length.

Then draw a second arrow that points right to add or left to subtract.

You can add or subtract on a number line.

HOME ACTIVITY Measure the lengths of a fork and a spoon in centimeters. Then draw a number line to show how you would find the total length of the two objects.

$10 + 19 = ?$

$10 + 19 = \underline{29}$

$19 - 13 = ?$

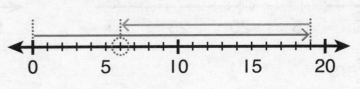

$19 - 13 = \underline{6}$

 Use the number lines to add or subtract.

1. $31 - 24 = $ _____

2. $18 + 23 = $ _____

3. **Number Sense** Look at the number line. Write the equation that it shows.

_____ ◯ _____ = _____

4. One box has 15 centimeters of ribbon.
Another box has 14 centimeters of ribbon.
How many centimeters of ribbon are in
both boxes?

_____ centimeters

5. Susan kicks a ball 26 yards to Joe.
Then, Joe kicks the ball 18 yards straight
back to Susan. How far is the ball from
Susan now?

_____ yards

6. **Higher Order Thinking** Henry is painting a 38-foot fence.
He paints 17 feet in the morning. He paints 16 more feet after
lunch. How many feet of fence are still left to paint?

You can draw
a number line
to help.

_____ feet

7. ☑ **Assessment Practice** Sam has 38 inches
of yarn. He gives 23 inches of yarn to Lars.
How many inches of yarn does Sam have
now? Show your work on the number line.

_____ inches

Copyright © Savvas Learning Company LLC. All Rights Reserved.

Name _____

Another Look! What tool would you use to solve this problem?

Valerie drives 21 miles on Monday and 49 miles on Tuesday. How many miles does she drive in all?

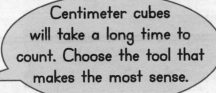
Centimeter cubes will take a long time to count. Choose the tool that makes the most sense.

You can draw a number line to solve this problem.

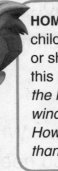

HOME ACTIVITY Ask your child to explain what tool he or she would use to solve this problem: *Measure the height of a door and a window to the nearest foot. How much taller is the door than the window?*

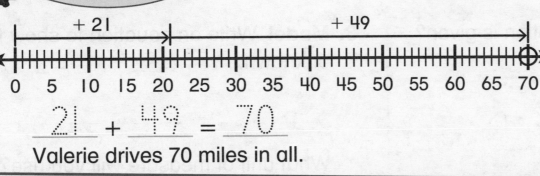

+ 21   + 49

0 5 10 15 20 25 30 35 40 45 50 55 60 65 70

__21__ + __49__ = __70__

Valerie drives 70 miles in all.

Choose a tool to help you solve the problem. Show your work. Explain why you chose that tool and how you got your answer.

1. Aaron was 38 inches tall when he was 4 years old. Aaron is 8 years old and 47 inches tall. How many inches did Aaron grow?

Trains

Mr. Bolt needs to measure the length of a train.
The first car is the engine car. It is 8 meters long.
There are also four boxcars. Each boxcar is
12 meters long.

Help Mr. Bolt find the total length of the train.

2. **Make Sense** What information is given?
What do you need to find?

_____

_____

_____

_____

3. **Model** Write an equation to show the
unknown.

_____

What unit of measure will you use?

_____

4. **Use Tools** What is the total length of the train?
Choose a tool to solve the problem. Show your work. _____

Copyright © Savvas Learning Company LLC. All Rights Reserved.

Name _____

Another Look! You can make a line plot to show data.

The table shows the lengths of objects in inches.
Use the data from the table to make a line plot.

HOME ACTIVITY Use the line plot to ask your child questions about the data. Encourage your child to explain each answer.

Object	Length in Inches
Pencil	5
Scissors	8
Stapler	6

The line plot helps you see how the lengths of the objects compare.

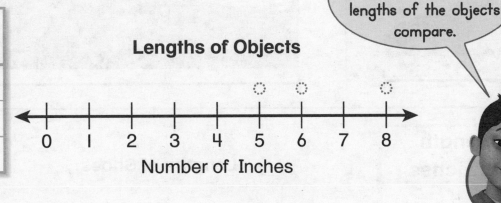

Lengths of Objects

Number of Inches
0 1 2 3 4 5 6 7 8

Use the line plot above to answer the questions.

1. How long is the shortest object? _____

2. How long is the longest object? _____

3. How much shorter is the shortest object than the longest object? _____ inches

4. What is the total length of all the objects? _____ inches

Be Precise Measure each shoe picture in inches. Then record each length in the table. Show each length in the table on the line plot.

5. This sneaker is

_____ long.

6. This dressy shoe is

_____ long.

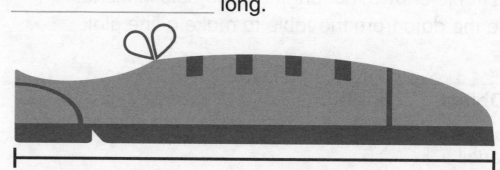

7.

Shoe Type	Length in Inches
Sandal	4
Loafer	5
Sneaker	
Dressy	

Lengths of Shoes

```
  ←――|――|――|――|――|――|――|――→
     0  1  2  3  4  5  6
```

Number of Inches

8. Higher Order Thinking Which three shoes have a total length of 13 inches? Explain.

_____

_____

9. ☑ **Assessment Practice** Measure the length of this leather shoe in inches. Write the length below. Record your measurement on the line plot above.

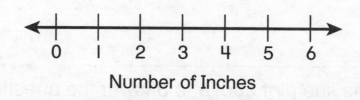

_____

Copyright © Savvas Learning Company LLC. All Rights Reserved.
Topic 15 | Lesson 1

Practice Video Tools Games

Another Look! 7 students measured the length of these scissors to the nearest centimeter. The results are shown in the table below.

Length of Scissors in Centimeters			
8	7	7	6
7	6	7	7

HOME ACTIVITY Have your child measure the lengths of three windows in your home. The windows should have different lengths. Then ask your child to make a line plot of the data.

Step 1 Measure the length of the scissors to the nearest centimeter.

Step 2 Write your measurement in the table above.

Step 3 Record your measurement on the line plot at the right.

Length of Scissors

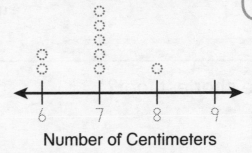

Number of Centimeters

Use the line plot above to answer each question.

1. Which measurement of the length of the scissors is most common?

_____ centimeters

2. Which could be different reasons students got different measurements? Write Yes or No.

_____ The object has a shape that is **NOT** flat.

_____ The measurement was halfway between two units.

_____ The ruler was not aligned with 0 when used.

Model Measure the foot length of 3 friends or family members. Write the measurements in the table below. Then use the data to complete the line plot.

3.

Foot Lengths in Inches			
8	7	8	7
6	9	6	7
10	7	9	10
7			

Foot Lengths

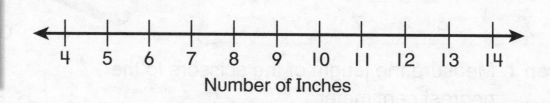

Number of Inches

---

4. How long is the shortest foot?

_____

5. What is the most common foot length?

_____

---

6. Higher Order Thinking How many people have a foot length that is an even number of inches? Explain.

_____

_____

_____

_____

7. ☑ **Assessment Practice** Measure the length of this foot to the nearest inch. Write the length below. Record your measurement on the line plot you made in Item 3.

_____ inches

Copyright © Savvas Learning Company LLC. All Rights Reserved.

Practice Video Tools Games

Another Look! A picture graph uses pictures or symbols to show information.

The numbers on the right tell how many students chose each snack. Complete the picture graph.

There are 9 symbols for popcorn. So 9 students chose popcorn.

HOME ACTIVITY Tell your child which snack shown in the picture graph is your favorite. Ask him or her to explain how the Favorite Snacks picture graph would change if your response was added to the picture graph.

Favorite Snacks		
Popcorn	☺☺☺☺☺☺☺☺☺	9
Fruit Cup	☺☺☺☺	4
Yogurt	☺☺☺☺☺☺☺	7
Cheese and Crackers	☺☺☺☺☺☺☺☺☺☺	10

Each ☺ = I student

Use the picture graph above to solve the problems.

1. How many students like cheese and crackers best? _____

2. How many students like yogurt best?
_____

3. How many more students like popcorn than fruit cups? _____ more students

4. Which snack is most students' favorite?
_____

Solve each problem.

5. Model The tally chart shows how many tickets each student has. Use the tally chart to complete the picture graph.

Tickets We Have	
Denise	IIII
Steve	II
Tom	卌 IIII
Lisa	卌 I

Tickets We Have	
Denise	
Steve	
Tom	
Lisa	

Each 🎫 = I ticket

6. Higher Order Thinking Lisa gives 2 tickets to Steve. How many tickets does Steve have now? Explain.

_____

_____

_____

7. ☑ Assessment Practice The tally chart shows the favorite pets of a class of second graders. Use the tally chart to draw a picture graph.

Favorite Pets	
Cat	卌 I
Dog	卌 II
Fish	卌
Hamster	II

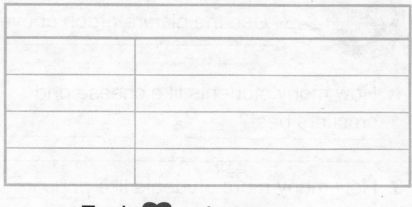

Each ♥ = I vote

Copyright © Savvas Learning Company LLC. All Rights Reserved.

Practice Video Tools Games

Another Look! You can draw conclusions from data in a graph.

This picture graph shows students' favorite types of books.
Write how many students chose each type of book.

The key shows that each book is 1 student's vote. Use the key to count the number of votes.

HOME ACTIVITY Use the Favorite Type of Book picture graph to ask your child questions about the data. Encourage your child to explain each answer.

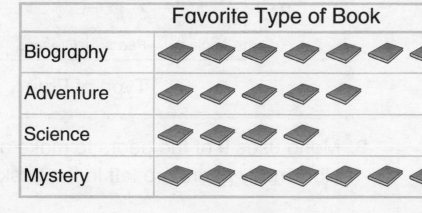

7

5

4

9

Favorite Type of Book	
Biography	📘📘📘📘📘📘📘
Adventure	📘📘📘📘📘
Science	📘📘📘📘
Mystery	📘📘📘📘📘📘📘📘📘

Each 📘 = 1 vote

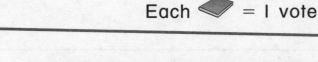

Use the picture graph above to answer the questions.

1. Which was the least favorite type of book?

_____

2. Which type of book did most students vote for? _____

3. How many more students voted for biography than for adventure?

_____ more students

4. If each student voted one time only, how many students voted in all?

Use the bar graph to solve each problem.

5. Make Sense Complete each sentence.

The fruit basket has _____ apples and _____ pears.

The fruit basket has _____ oranges and _____ plums.

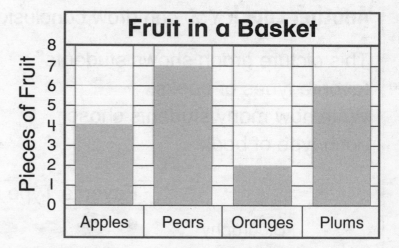

6. Write the order of the type of fruit from the least number to the greatest number.

_____

7. How many apples and oranges are in the basket in all?

_____

8. Maria uses 4 of the pears to make a pie. How many pears are left in the basket?

_____

9. Higher Order Thinking Does it matter how you order the data in a bar graph? Explain.

_____

_____

_____

10. ☑ **Assessment Practice** Look at the bar graph in Item 5. How many more plums than apples are in the basket?

_____ more plums

Copyright © Savvas Learning Company LLC. All Rights Reserved.
Topic 15 | Lesson 5

Name _____

Another Look! You can reason about data in the picture graph to write and solve problems.

How many more votes did the Tigers get than the Lions?

Votes for Team Name	
Wolves	🧍🧍🧍🧍🧍
Tigers	🧍🧍🧍🧍🧍🧍🧍🧍🧍🧍
Lions	🧍🧍🧍🧍🧍🧍🧍🧍

Each 🧍 = 1 vote

Count the symbols for the votes for Tigers and Lions on the picture graph. Then subtract.

Tigers __10__   Lions __8__

__10__ – __8__ = __2__

The Tigers got __2__ more votes than the Lions.

HOME ACTIVITY Look at the picture graph for team names together. Ask your child to find how many more votes there are for Wolves and Lions combined than there are for Tigers. Have your child explain how to find the answer.

Write and solve problems about the data in the picture graph above.

1. _____

_____

____ ◯ ____ = ____

_____

2. _____

_____

____ ◯ ____ = ____

_____

Gym Games

Ms. Winn has to cut one game from gym class. So, she asked students to choose their favorite game. The bar graph shows the results. Each student voted only once. Which game should she cut and why?

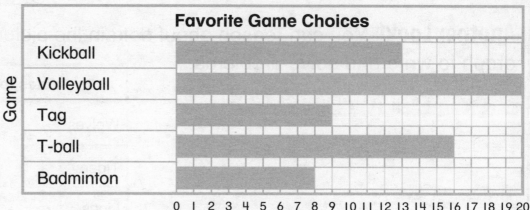

Favorite Game Choices

3. **Make Sense** How many students voted for each game? Tell how you know.

_____

_____

_____

4. **Explain** Ms. Winn thinks tag should be taken out of gym class. Do you agree? Explain.

_____

_____

_____

_____

5. **Reasoning** How many fewer students chose tag and badminton combined than volleyball? Explain your reasoning.

_____

_____

_____

_____

Copyright © Savvas Learning Company LLC. All Rights Reserved.

Photographs

Every effort has been made to secure permission and provide appropriate credit for photographic material. The publisher deeply regrets any omission and pledges to correct errors called to its attention in subsequent editions.

Unless otherwise acknowledged, all photographs are the property of Savvas Learning Company LLC.

170 Optionm/Shutterstock; **214** Ivan Kruk/Fotolia.